Hereward College

LEARNING RESOURCES

CENTRE

INDIA

with Sanjeev Bhaskar

INDIA

with Sanjeev Bhaskar

To my parents and the generation
that travelled the longest road to get
to the farthest shore.

HarperCollins*Publishers*

HarperCollins*Publishers*
77–85 Fulham Palace Road,
Hammersmith, London W6 8JB

www.harpercollins.co.uk

First published in 2007 by HarperCollins*Publishers*
1

BBC logo © BBC 2007
The BBC logo is a registered trademark of the
British Broadcasting Corporation and is used
under their licence

Written by Sanjeev Bhaskar and Deep Sehgal
Copyright © Sanjeev Bhaskar and Deep Sehgal

The author asserts the moral right to
be identified as the author of this work

A CIP catalogue record for this book
is available from the British Library

ISBN-10   0-00-724738-9
ISBN-13   978-0-00-724738-7

Printed and bound in Great Britain
by Butler and Tanner, Somerset

CONTENTS

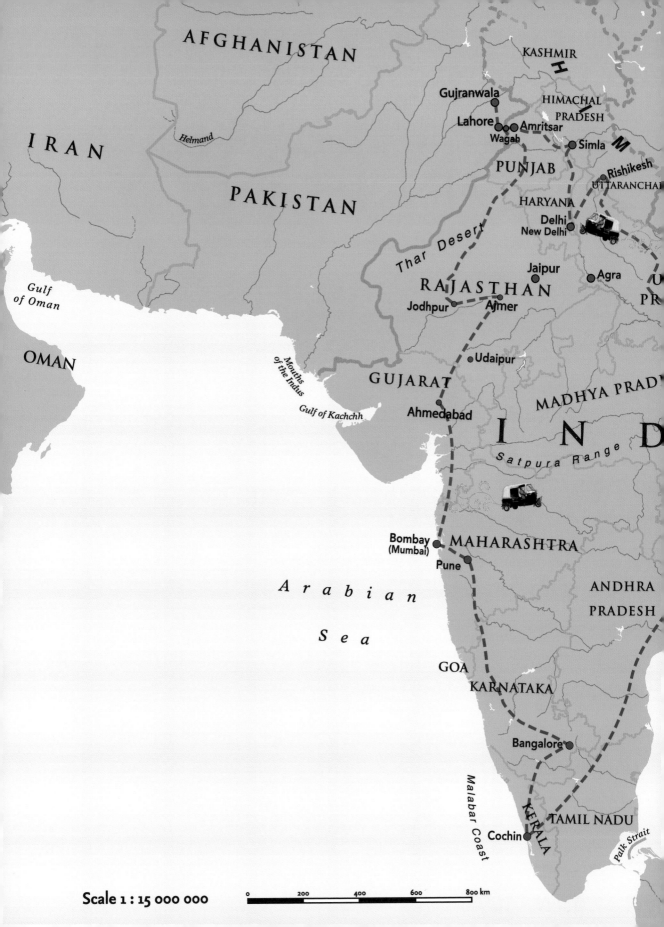

INTRODUCTION

Looking for India

Where I grew up, my family home in a west London suburb was hardly salubrious. My parents, sister and I lived in a small terraced maisonette above a launderette. No, it wasn't my beautiful launderette. It was my father's, and it wasn't especially beautiful either.

We had no central heating, making do with a couple of gas fires and a paraffin heater to stave off those arctic winters of the 1960s. A water tank with the capacity of about a pint served our washing and bathing needs and our windows were the wrong size for that new fad, double-glazing. My Dad improvised by nailing thick polythene sheets to the inside of the windows to thwart the convectional currents of cold air that would pass through the windows like evil spectres.

Our flat had no garden and my summers were spent staring out of the window at the main road and devouring as many books as my dog-eared library card would allow. To top it all, we were directly under one of the main flight paths in to Heathrow Airport, which meant that even casual conversation contained a cliffhanger every few minutes: 'You know, Auntie Manju deserves a slap ... [Plane] ... up meal for giving Mr Ram a servicing ... [Plane] ... contract for all his shag ... [Plane] ... pile carpets, 'cos it's a right bugger ... [Plane] ... to clean.'

Was there a silver lining to living in this dark, dank cloud? Well, perhaps a couple. Next door was a fish 'n' chip shop run by Auntie

BELOW: A stylish 4-year-old author (complete with foot-straps on the pants) outside his father's launderette in Heston, west London.

9

Phyllis and Uncle Gordon, who were warm, funny and regularly provided me with my hourly fix of chips. When the weather turned nasty, our whole family would decamp to the living room for a couple of weeks, which was as close as we ever came to a camping holiday. And we were perfectly placed for getting to and from the airport, of course.

My mother filled much of my childhood with stories about her childhood. Tales of my relatives which all took place in exotic locations in India. I heard about floods and earthquakes, cobras and leopards. Trapping fire flies in jars and munching on raw sugar cane. Travelling by steam trains and riding in rickshaws. Maharajas and mahouts. A series of saturated, Kodachrome snapshots of my mother's past.

For all her lurid memories, in the background were the shadows of Partition. This was the violent and bloody separation of Old India which took place in 1947 – cleaving the British Empire's most precious jewel and marking the birth of the conjoined twins of Pakistan and modern India. The stories always became sparse at this point, fading to a whisper and then finally to silent introspection.

My father worked shifts at a local factory. This meant he was on a constant cycle of changing work times: 6 a.m. till 2 p.m., 2 p.m. till 10 p.m. and 10 p.m. till 6 a.m. This was six days a week and, in between, he was running the launderette too. The fact that my father survived this occupational assault, and indeed prospered, is an achievement that I now hold in the highest regard, but as a child I viewed with naïve derision.

This was primarily because my sister and I had to learn to remain mute during different parts of the day when he was resting. This enforced semi-monastic existence ill-prepared me for the sensual onslaught that visiting India would bring. It also meant that I heard little from my father about his childhood, save for the hardship that came early to him after his father died just before Partition – from what I understand were health problems brought about by an excessive work ethic.

Though my father's childhood stories were rare to my ears, even they subsided when the subject of Partition came up, at which point he would either go to work, bed or silently disappear behind a newspaper.

All I knew about Partition from both my parents was that it was horrendous, that the family somehow survived, and that my father's family lost everything and came to Delhi as refugees.

Saturday night in west London was the Indian social night. A merry band of my parents and their friends would congregate in someone's house on a rota basis. This was the surrogate extended family that all of these NRIs (Non Resident Indians) seemed to have hankered for.

Inevitably all of them had little family in the UK and so the week-end was the smash-and-grab opportunity for them to get their *desi* familial fix before returning to the not-altogether-warm welcome of daily English life.

Spices, herbs and fruit from Mother India were not readily available (a curry being something that came out of a packet to which you added boiling water – and, by enforcement of some diabolical by-law, had to contain sultanas) and so food from 'home' was understandably precious.

A guest always revealed a mango or some okra in a very dramatic fashion, like a Victorian illusionist, punctuated by the audience's 'Oohs' and 'Ahs', culminating in the gentle thud of someone fainting. To this day I still sense an endorphin rush around exotic fruit.

The chatter during these evenings would build to a crescendo timed perfectly to peak with the arrival of the last guest. Then chat gave way to the harmonium and the raucous singing of traditional and *filmi* songs. As social exhaustion set in, the songs would turn melancholic and all the adults would in turn lose themselves in some unified memory of personal loss, though *Partition* was never ever spoken of.

My parents and their friends imparted to me two visions of India. One was a rosy pre-Partition vista of innocent wide-eyed endearment. Images of play, wonder and hope. These were still the days of the British Raj, when Gandhi urged a radical new approach that was inspiring the masses. Leaders like Jawaharlal Nehru were urging the people to push this foetal nation down the birthing canal towards the light of independence. After several hundred years, India was finally to be free and all that that small four-letter word implies. There was so much hope.

The other vision of India was of a country rent in two by upheaval and hardship, confusion and hurt. India post-Independence. This was the India of the melancholic song, of friends, family and land that my parents and many of their peers would never see again. The realization that freedom does indeed come at a price. A free India that they were forced to desert in order to survive.

So even though I was an easy-going kid, albeit with a fear of large loud groups of Indian people, the announcement of an impending trip to the old country always filled me with excited apprehension. Perhaps this time I was going to encounter some small pocket of *old* India, the India of hope and ideals?

However, hope was all I ever took with me in my small grey suitcase and when I returned to England, it would still be lying there underneath my maroon Y-fronts and crisp white vests. I only ever seemed to meet the *new* India of discord and confusion.

These long holidays were spent with my family in the capital city of New Delhi. My widowed paternal grandmother lived on the third floor in a tenement flat, which consisted of two rooms and a small polished granite area that doubled as a makeshift kitchen and bathroom. The communal toilets were outside the flat along the communal hall. She shared these living quarters with my widowed aunt *and* her three children. When we pitched up, the already scarce floor space totally disappeared. In those days the mains water supply only ran until 9 a.m., so my grandmother would wake at 6 a.m. and fill plastic buckets with enough cold water for the day.

Even to an easy-going kid from west London, those long, hot vacations seemed like an almost sadistic catalogue of discomforts and inconveniences. Water was precious, electricity was scarce and power cuts were frequent and spontaneous. Mosquitoes dive-bombed with gay abandon, strafing exposed skin at every opportunity, and even the flies added a swagger to their flight. Everything smelled of gasoline, melting tarmac, cow dung and heat. Air conditioning and telephones were reserved for the *very* rich. Needless to say, computers did not exist.

OPPOSITE: Haven't you heard? Colours are in this year ... in fact, in India they are every year.

12

ABOVE: 'Bollywood' – India's film industry. Some of the movies today make more money outside India than within.

So, from an easy-going kid I grew to become a hormonally confused adolescent and then a curious young adult. But even today, those regular visits we made to India as I grew up resolutely refuse to be consigned to poetic memory. The country remains consistently baffling.

This is the same country that, only twenty years later, is reported to lead the world in biotechnology and pharmaceutical research, has the world's largest radio telescope array and is undergoing a renaissance that will confirm its place at the centre of global politics. Something doesn't ring true. How can this be?

Incredibly, it would seem that India is being reborn before our very eyes. But how on earth has it managed to transform itself from an impoverished colony into a global leader so quickly? How can a country with more than a billion citizens lead itself, let alone the world? Why did I need to speak to somebody in Bangalore when I wanted to get from London to Paddington – and can his name really be Bunny?

These and countless other questions require further investigation.

June 2006

Amongst strange shadowy shapes I sit up sleepily, slightly confused. Am I awake? My surroundings come into focus and the sight of a large man, snoring away, dribble happily glistening down the side of his mouth like tinsel, reminds me exactly where I am.

Boeing 747, seat 35C. Thirty-five thousand feet below us, the ocean's deep blue surface is gently rippled and pockmarked like the skin of a tangerine. As we push onwards into a cloudless and brightening sky, I begin to consider the enormity of the journey ahead. I am now visiting India again, but this time the insatiable curiosity of my youth has a new lens to view it through – I have a BBC film crew with me. This time, I'm documenting my quest to find where old India meets new India, meets the *real* India.

ABOVE: Trying to look cool and avoiding the embarrassment of handing the stewardess a sick bag.

As India approaches her 60th birthday, our mission is both exhilarating and daunting: to somehow get under the skin of this enormous, lumbering nation, a country that against all the odds is rapidly emerging as a global superpower.

The first warning signs started to appear in British newspapers about ten years ago. Did we know, asked the alarming headlines, that India was becoming a silent partner to our high-street institutions? Banks, airlines, insurance companies, even the international stock markets were beginning to depend on computer programmers based somewhere in India.

But those intriguing headlines were only a tiny part of the story, and the Indian revolution was only just beginning. A decade later and it's in full steam (although for a nuclear power that may be an outmoded reference). So, will I even be able to recognize the place?

As the 747's wheels platonically kiss Indian soil, a clipped English voice welcomes us to *Hindustan*. Even before the cabin doors have gone to manual, the smells of kerosene, damp earth and disinfectant filter through the ventilators and the atmosphere of India begins to enter our systems.

PART ONE

INDIA CALLING

CHAPTER ONE

Bombay Dreams

As I enter the cool, modern, marble immigration hall, I have a familiar sinking feeling, knowing that I cannot compete with my pre-ordained destiny of joining the slowest-moving line. An expressionless khaki-uniformed guard ushers me to a booth, where I wait patiently behind the yellow line as the vociferous family in front of me remonstrate with an unperturbed official. As I glance around me I see several hundred passengers resignedly shuffling forward like some huge chain gang.

However, as I emerge having had my papers stamped I am swept into a torrent of people, holdalls and pushchairs competing in the luggage sprint. As we enter the baggage hall, the frenzied pace quickens as trolleys now also join the fray. A wobbling Punjabi lady rockets past me. Her three young boys sit in single file on the trolley, their bowl haircuts looking like crash helmets and the whole tableau reminiscent of a bobsleigh team in full pelt. The mass urgency is about finding the prime position in the next contest: 'Whose Bag Is It Anyway?'

It's nearly 6 a.m., and we're waiting for our luggage outside Mumbai's International Airport. An endless procession of filming equipment continues to emerge from the baggage hall. A group of porters in light blue shirts and bare feet are fighting over our custom. They rush back and forth frenetically, squawking like crows.

OPPOSITE: Bombay. City of Dreams.

Eventually all of the equipment is checked, tagged, stacked and loaded into a blue Maruti van. The porters *salaam* as they each receive ten rupees, and we finally begin the long drive into Mumbai.

Beside the new expressway runs an untarmacked track. A bustling shanty town has sprung up alongside the old airport road, and although the sun has only recently risen, for the inhabitants of the suburbs the new day is clearly under way. Oblivious to the traffic whizzing past only inches away, bright orange saris are topped with ebony faces, carved figureheads with silver nose-rings and inscrutable expressions.

Bombay's traffic, like that of all the major Indian cities experiencing the twin gifts of galloping prosperity and ambling infrastructure, is a white-knuckle experience. Every manner of conveyance jostles for minuscule advantage on the crowded roadways. Jeremy Clarkson once referred to it as 'The Hindu Code'. Basically it works like this: if your vehicle is smaller than mine, then you better watch it, mate. It's always the responsibility of the person behind. So if someone cuts in front of you, you better make damn sure you don't hit him. Experienced drivers suddenly discover invisible chicanes, swinging their cars around like they're between Paris and Dakar, rather than on the main highway

RIGHT: Road sense is slowly seeping into India's traffic consciousness. Little children are no longer allowed to take the rest of the family out for a ride.

OPPOSITE: The black and yellow taxis of Bombay look like lethargic bees as they crawl through the commuting traffic jams.

from the international airport, heading downtown. In the heady melange of trucks, buses, cars, scooters, three-wheeler 'tuk tuks' and some vehicles that defy any description whatsoever, I'm amazed that there are no collisions.

On the rare occasions that we come to a stop, we are serenaded by the street people. An impossibly young child carrying an impossibly younger child, taps on the window and wearily trots out her begging routine. What she's saying is unintelligible but the message is pretty clear. Within a few moments she spies a sleek foreign car with tinted windows and is off for richer pickings. Then the hawkers arrive. A flotilla of unnecessary gaudily coloured knick-knacks are promenaded before our closed windows. Plastic wind fans, lighters, small inflatable elephants, postcards and, even more improbably, Jeffery Archer's back catalogue are all proffered with varying degrees of disinterest. My mind drifts towards the rare person who exclaims 'Oh, thank God! *First Among Equals* and an inflatable elephant, exactly what I needed!'

Finally I spy one of the quintessential Indian sights. I see my first cow, nonchalantly picking her way across a line of impatient traffic, like a general at a passing-out parade.

This is the India of my memory, and on first impressions, out here in the suburbs little seems to have changed since my visits as a youngster. I'm told that today India has the world's 11th largest economy, and yet it's still home to a quarter of the world's poorest people. Will India ever be able to bring the benefits of the bright and shining new millennium to her entire population, or have India's rich and poor simply learned to ignore each other more efficiently?

From my privileged vantage point here in the van, just twelve hours after leaving Heathrow it's already clear to me that over the coming weeks mind-scrambling contrasts and inconsistencies will present themselves at every turn. Skyscrapers and slums, nuclear-power stations and emaciated farmers in dusty fields. The bulging train into the city hobbles past, bursting at the seams with early-morning commuters holding on for dear life.

Bombay (or Mumbai as it's been somewhat pointlessly renamed) is at the very heart of India's reawakening. This is, after all, the financial capital of the country, and if there's one place that embodies the spirit of the new India it's got to be Bombay.

This is India's city of superlatives, where glamour and grinding poverty are equally ubiquitous. Maximum City. City of Dreams. Metropolis. An appropriate point to start my epic and slightly daunting voyage across the modern subcontinent.

While Delhi might manage the politics and Calcutta is reputed to be the intellectual, spiritual heart of the country, it's Bombay that you come to if you want to make your fortune. Here every waiter in the surprisingly sleek upmarket coffee bars and eateries is an aspiring movie star and the city is well known for being home to the world's largest film industry. It's no coincidence that Bombay more than any other Indian city is the city of dreams. People come here with a Dick Whittington vision of streets paved with gold, and for a happy few this turns out to be true.

I spend my first morning with Gautam Singhania, one of India's wealthiest men and heir to the Raymond Empire. When I was a child, driving through the streets of India one of the most common sights would be rather lurid red neon lettering that said 'Raymond'. It didn't say anything else, I just thought it was advertising a guy called Raymond – but it transpires that Raymond is one of the country's largest textile manufacturing companies and Gautam Singhania is heir to this fortune.

Today they have more than four hundred stores in cities all over the country but their centre of operations is very much Bombay, and this is Gautam's city. My visit started with a chopper ride – it was the first time I had ever been up in a helicopter and I'm already looking forward to the return leg. From this vantage point one begins to get a sense of the city's development. The skyscrapers which are already beginning to dominate the city skyline mingle with older colonial apartments and throw long shadows over the telltale corrugated-iron-roofed shacks of the needy.

Our destination was Thane, an industrial district a couple of hours drive north of the city. Only a twenty-minute chopper ride away, the factory there is at the heart of the Raymond manufacturing empire.

Much has been made of India's recent economic boom but it's when you're actually on the ground that you realize why India's future looks so promising, and it's to do with the sheer number of people available to work.

The factory looks like it hasn't much changed since the 1950s. An endless line of workers queue up patiently to punch in before going to their stations. Inside it's dimly lit. In a cavernous space roughly the size of a football pitch, thousands of women are painstakingly examining every inch of fabric that's produced here.

'No machine can beat eyes and fingers,' says Gautam. 'We don't need a separate quality control department – it's done at every stage. The workers first look for blemishes and then also run their hands over the material and this happens at every stage, so we can guarantee that we use only the best material.'

The quality of the material made here is quite astonishing; the most expensive fabric in the world is made in this very building. A suit made from it, Gautam tells me with pride, will cost me 10,000 dollars. I silently visualize the contents of my wallet. 'Maybe next time,' I tell him. All the while, I can hear the distant thrum of heavy machinery.

Over lunch, Gautam explains that it's the enormous available Indian workforce that's given the company such an advantage over its competitors in the West, and introduces me to some of the oldest serving members of staff, octogenarians who proudly announce that they've never worked anywhere else.

'Mr Gautam's father employed me,' one of them tells me. 'I remember Mr Gautam, when he was a little boy, accompanying his father to the factory.'

'You must've noticed some changes in Gautam over the years,' I say.

'Yes,' said the old chap. 'He got older.'

BELOW: Bollywood's glamorous Shilpa Shetty. If you want to chat up a beautiful Indian girl, best learn the right dance moves – else that could be you they're all laughing at.

Since India's economy opened up to foreign investment in the early 1990s, Raymond has entered into international agreements with companies across the globe, a dramatic change of direction for a company first established in 1925 and which signals India's modern outward-looking philosophy. Gautam proudly informs me that his company is a world leader in worsted suits. I nod, sagely disguising the fact that I don't know what 'worsted' means.

For your information, from the Oxford English Dictionary:

worsted /woostid/• noun 1 a fine smooth yarn spun from long strands of combed wool. 2 fabric made from such yarn.

BELOW: Skyscrapers and slums. The white building in the foreground (far left) has been built to house the people living in the slum at its base. But have the dwellers ever been higher than the ground floor?

Our time at the factory is brief as we have a very tight schedule – and the next stage of our journey is made in a chauffeur-driven Mercedes. Within arm's reach are miniature bottles of Evian and Gautam's driver looks a lot smarter than I do this morning.

We're heading to the Atria Mall, one of Bombay's newest and spangliest shopping emporiums, where Gautam has promised to get me

kitted out for the evening's festivities. Tonight, aboard his private yacht, Gautam is throwing a party for me, the crew and a few local billionaires.

I feel like a character in one of those cheesy American movies as I step out of the dressing room in a variety of different guises. None of them quite feel right. How are you supposed to dress for a party of billionaires? I settle on a rather subtle stripy shirt and a pair of anonymous-looking chinos. This is a look that has become surprisingly popular in the new India – out with the stay-pressed flares and the Brylcreem, and in with the Gap and Armani and all the other labels that are familiar from home.

ABOVE: My first helicopter ride with Gautam Singhania. Note the fashionable iPod headphones.

As we leave the air-conditioned comfort of the Atria Mall, we make an impromptu stop at the Rolls-Royce showroom next door. I suspect that the lone vehicle standing gleaming like some celestial chariot is the only one they have in stock. Gautam tells me that over the past year over 700 Porsches and many Ferraris have been purchased in India. Having experienced Indian roads I wonder where they could possibly be driven?

'Many aren't driven at all,' Gautam tells me. 'They're status symbols, some guys just like the thought that they own one … it's an indication of the kind of money that's being made in India at the moment.'

I ask him what's brought about this change of attitude in a country where, whenever I had visited as a child, an imported car was only really seen in the movies.

'Labels have become important. People in the business sector are very aware that commerce has become globally interdependent. They do business with foreign companies, go abroad a lot more than the previous generation did, watch television, access the world wide web and they want to show the world that Indians are the equal of anybody, including buying the brands that are globally acknowledged as status symbols.'

This makes sense to me as the number of smart shops in these rapidly multiplying malls are selling the kind of designer wares that were seen as exclusive European chic only a couple of decades back, and practically unobtainable in India. Today, from watches to running shoes to laptops to mobile phones (and of course luxury cars), they are available at your local mall. Even Marks and Spencer is available for those needing an exotic injection of western commercialism.

Gautam then made me an offer I simply couldn't refuse. Would I like another chopper ride, this time to his 'chill out' pad to freshen up before the evening's soirée? I blurted out an emotional 'yes' before he'd finished the sentence. Fifteen minutes later, after a spectacular trip across the bay, we land at a helipad secreted amongst palm trees. Another ten minutes on, after driving through dense verdant terrain, we arrive at two large wooden gates, eerily reminiscent of *Jurassic Park*. Blanched-uniformed attendants snap to a salute and, on opening the gates, reveal a large whitewashed Spanish-villa-styled building. We walk through to a huge thatched open-sided barn which houses a snooker table, wicker chairs and a fully stocked bar, all impressively reflected in the marble floor.

I'm offered refreshments while Gautam taps at a computer terminal at the bar. At first I assume he's closing yet another international deal, until I realize he's changing the music, gently wafting down from the bar's loudspeakers.

After showering and changing in the plush guest quarters, I decide to have a wander around the grounds. Between the buildings and the calm Arabian Sea is the irregularly shaped swimming pool, replete with sunken bar, but with that extra touch of extravagance: Jacuzzi jets. This small detail encapsulates the fact that for a certain, rarefied strata of Indian society money can buy anything the heart desires.

Refreshed and slightly awestruck, after another short drive I find myself at an anonymous-looking jetty. At the end of it idles a speedboat, which we leap into and Gautam whizzes us across the pretty, natural bay which gave Bombay both its name and its fortune. Bon Bay – Bombay.

Zipping across the waves at frightening speed, we rapidly approach our destination – an immaculately restored dhow boat, towering majestically above us with its sails in silhouette against the setting sun. This day seems to be turning into one long James Bond fantasy, and I have to confess that I'm loving every minute of it.

As I sip Moët while the sun sets over the Arabian Sea, I can't help but wonder just how removed I am from the real Bombay. Still, it's only day one, and the next few days will give me a chance to get beneath the city's glamorous veneer. Gautam's yacht deposits me at my hotel and I sleep soundly, dreaming of gadgets, girls and gabardine.

ABOVE: Women praying at Juhu Beach, Mumbai. Hindus believe that God is everywhere and this lot are convinced that he's even in that pedalo just out of shot in the Arabian Sea.

Two worlds collide

The Mumbai municipal corporations have to deal with all the issues of maintaining one of the most populated cities in the world. Hence, the infrastructure is always struggling to keep pace with Bombay's estimated 18 million people. I had heard that small private ventures were plugging the gaps where the state mechanism could sometimes not cope. One of these areas was just rubbish. No seriously, I mean garbage collection. Most of central Bombay, just like central London or central New York or central anywhere, is made up of high-rise blocks in which the middle classes live. As the day breaks there's a fairly pleasant and languid atmosphere. It's a very relaxed winter's morning just like any other except for a rather shrill call that pierces the air.

The massive Victoria Terminus in Mumbai. Better maintained than St Pancras and lots of civil servants looking like Harry Potter.

'Piparè!' A long pause.

'Piparè!'

The sound appears to be coming from over the garden wall, and when I investigate the source I find that it's emanating from a very, very small hunchback. It's surprising he has the lungs for it. He's carrying a cloth sack on one shoulder and a tiny rucksack on the other. He looks for all the world like one of Santa's little helpers or a character in a surrealist French movie.

A few moments later he's joined by a maid from the tower block. She's carrying a neat bundle of newspapers and seven or eight empty plastic canisters. What looks like a heated argument ensues, both haggling wildly over the price of, well, rubbish. One of the residents of the tower block kindly agreed to explain what the hell is going on …

It turns out that all over the city at dawn, thousands of people leave their homes and make their way to the more affluent suburbs in order to clear their rubbish. But they aren't paid by the municipal authorities;

30

these people are free agents. Bombay is basically kept clean by a vast army of rag-and-bone men who buy and sell the city's rubbish. The rubbish is carefully sorted, then packaged into large bundles for sale.

Recycling, Indian style.

This particular rag picker, who specializes in newspapers, is known only as 'hunchback', which is either terribly politically incorrect, or a phenomenal coincidence. Once his morning rounds were done he allowed me to follow him to a street called Arab Gully where he sells his reclaimed garbage.

Here, everything from tin cans, bottles, newspapers and plastic up to car batteries and even entire taxi cabs is broken down, stripped to its constituent parts and then sold to the highest bidder. Amazing when you consider that in the West we spend billions of pounds trying to encourage people to recycle. In India they look after the paisa, and the rupees take care of themselves.

As I walk to the end of Arab Gully, in the distance I can see a pair of half-constructed skyscrapers. They're called Imperial Towers, and the flats that they contain are so luxurious that they won't even tell me how much they cost. It's often cited that Bombay has higher real-estate prices than London, New York or Paris. It's a sign of our modern paranoid times that I can't help being slightly unnerved by the sight of the twin towers, which are aimed to be the tallest in India. Will they become the lofty goals of India's super rich or simply the target of evildoers?

There is an attempt here to give commercial enterprise a conscience. Part of the deal that the Imperial Towers' owners have agreed to is to provide accommodation for the inhabitants of the small slum dwellings on its doorstep. To this end, a smaller tower has been built, without the high specifications and presidential security of its imposing twin brothers, naturally, but a respectable abode nevertheless. As I drive past these half-finished symbols of modern India I can't help thinking about how these poor folk, still shielded by so much corrugated iron and so used to living at, and often on, street level, will deal

with being perched on the twenty-fifth floor of a high-rise block? Something tells me they weren't consulted; yet here they still are, awaiting their notice of eviction from their carefully maintained hovels, but without any sense of bitterness.

No matter how many times you visit this country it's always baffling to see both of these worlds living beside one another – the rag pickers obliviously plying their trade at the end of a street which contains the most valuable real estate on the planet.

It occurs to me that this is the most difficult question I'm going to have to answer on this epic Indian journey of mine – why is it that India, with all of its extremes and contradictions, doesn't simply implode? As we crawl our way through traffic on our way back to the hotel I realize that this mission is going to be more difficult than I first thought.

Myths, melodrama and marriage

Storytelling has always been an important part of India's heritage. At first, purely an oral tradition, as the great Hindu epics, the *Mahabharata* and *Ramayana*, were passed down from generation to generation over a thousand-year period. In fact when the *Mahabharata*, thought to be the longest epic poem in the world, became a 94-episode television series in the late 1980s, it quickly became the first 'must-see' TV event in Indian history. The country came to a standstill every Sunday morning as did the populace, as hundreds crowded the living rooms and even the outside windows of those who had television sets. Thus began a love affair with television serials that involve moral dilemmas, subterfuge, families and melodrama. They're now known as soap operas and they're big. Really big.

I arrive in an anonymous Mumbai suburb called Andheri West and approach a rather glitzy-looking glass building that looks strangely out of place when you consider that it's surrounded by the usual Indian chaos. There's very little visible on the outside that would lead you to suspect that inside India's most popular soap opera is being filmed.

The star of the show is a rather gutsy woman called Smriti Iraani. Smriti's not your average thirty year old. Not content with being one of the most famous people in the world, with well over two hundred million avid fans watching her show every week, she's also got a political profile and in her dressing room there's a copy of Sonia Gandhi's autobiography just waiting to be leafed through.

She sits patiently while a team of hair and make-up artists transform her from her thirty-year-old self into the sixty-year-old that she plays on screen. Just one floor above us a team of maybe forty technicians are building the set and by the time Smriti's make-up's done, they're ready to shoot her close-ups. This is a purpose-built television studio, with dressing rooms, props store and administration offices. So I'm a little surprised to find that the set, one floor up, is actually on the roof. This is the closest we come to soundproofing. If you can't shut the sound out, move as far away from it as possible. In this case it means move as far above it as possible. The hum of vehicles, street hawkers, dogs barking and someone hitting a sheet of metal with a cat dim slightly but still reverberate around the eardrums.

Smriti plays the matriarch of a family going through crisis. The soap is called *Kyunki Saas Bhi Kabhi Bahu Thi* – or 'Because every mother-in-law was once a daughter-in-law'. Smriti plays 'Tulsi', the lead, a mother-in-law desperately fighting injustices within her in-laws' family. What makes this especially surreal is that Smriti joined the show some seven years ago, playing 'Tulsi', the eighteen-year-old new daughter-in-law … desperately fighting the injustices within her in-laws' family. So her character has aged over forty years in less than ten. In the wide berth of logic that are Indian soaps, the rest of the world – fashion, popular reference points, etc. – have remained resolutely contemporary, but almost a quarter of a billion viewers worldwide don't seem to be bothered by this mere footnote.

Smriti herself is a million miles from the dour and put-upon character she plays. She's smart, funny and very media savvy. A hushed reverence greets her as she gets into position to shoot her close-ups.

OVERLEAF: Bombay's Ganpati festival. Hindu holy days are numerous and never to be approached in a shy and retiring manner.

ABOVE: Smriti Iraani, star of the biggest soap opera in India. Humble and with a great sense of humour.

Every now and again, as if to add to the surreal nature of the experience, I hear someone whisper the word 'shoom' in the background. 'Shoom,' says the voice, 'shoom'. Each time I hear the whisper, the camera whips around madly only to re-find Smriti in the frame a few moments later.

It transpires that 'shoom' is the word that the young director has coined for this rather crazy form of camera movement, a kind of crash zoom that ends on Smriti's distraught features. The close-ups dispensed with, Smriti wanders over and asks me if I want to play a walk-on.

I jump at the chance of joining this surreal circus, if only for a day. The part she has given me is of a sleazy producer who walks up to her character and says, 'Are you a dancer?' Her character then calls me an idiot and walks away.

As I start to get into character I ask Smriti about the popularity of the programmes she appears in.

'Family is fundamental to Indian society, so social melodramas always hit home. Whereas movies were about escapism, television, being in people's homes, needed to touch on real life, so serials concerning desire versus duty, the difficulties in living in extended families and now the impact of children moving away to work and, of course, after marriage, of the daughter coming to live with the in-laws are all rich areas for drama.'

I ask her what kind of response she gets from her adoring public. Smriti laughs. 'Many people come up and sympathize and say "Why did you put up with so and so talking to you like that?" or they say they too went through something similar.'

I don a rather lary shirt, a set of gold medallions and I'm ready for my close-up now. The set is almost unbearably hot and there isn't time for introductions to the cast of extras, who are playing dancers. Meanwhile, to my left the human smoke machine is making the atmosphere a bit more, well, atmospheric. He's wearing a yoke across his back, and on either side are two metal crucibles filled with smoking incense. He runs around the set twice and – bingo – instant atmosphere.

The Indian soap industry has seen a boom in recent years. With a huge proliferation in the number of television channels available and a massive national appetite for melodrama, it seems to confirm the idea of modern India as a country of aspirations; with Bombay its creative capital.

As I drive away from the film set I find every available inch of space is covered with billboard hoardings. One of them is particularly intriguing. It's a picture of a very attractive set of women lying back on a bed of roses.

The caption runs 'Attractive, vivacious, married? Just what we're looking for', and an address follows. I decide to investigate this cryptic challenge a little further. This kind of advertising was unheard of on my previous visits.

The address belongs to a nondescript building with a repetition of the billboard hoarding outside. On the building itself is a flickering blue sign that reads 'Gladrags Modelling and Aviation Academy'. Aviation? I look round but see no planes, hang gliders or guys in goggles.

A steady stream of very attractive women are making their way into the building and I feel duty-bound to follow them. These are the semi-finals of the Mrs India Contest. Mrs India is no ordinary beauty pageant. The one qualifying criteria is that … you're married.

The contest is the brainchild of Maureen Wadia. Think Sharon Osbourne meets Tina Brown. Maureen is part of the Wadia family, the largest landowners in Bombay. Already spectacularly wealthy, Maureen is not interested in lounging by the pool with a cocktail.

We chat on the lawn outside the studio space as the girls ready themselves for their moment in the spotlight. Well, actually there's no spotlight, or television cameras (apart from ours), and no audience. A simple room with a judge's desk at one end and just a chair at the other.

'I wanted to show that Indian women don't lose any of their vitality, passion or looks after marriage. There's an idea that married women should just disappear and become subservient to their husbands, just

BELOW: As a sleazy producer in Smriti's soap. No acting required.

37

housewives and mothers. There's nothing wrong with that but it doesn't mean that's all we are.'

'But Maureen,' I ask, 'doesn't any kind of pageant, particularly one that involves beauty, just objectify women and reinforces them as sexual objects?'

Maureen flashes me a confident smile. 'You would rather see some blonde running down a beach in a bikini rather than an Indian girl in a sari ... I see.'

'No, no,' I protest. 'I'll happily watch a girl running down the beach in a deep sea diver's outfit. I'm not bothered what she's wearing, honestly.'

'But we are sexy and we are intelligent and we have a vital contribution to make to society,' Maureen replies, 'and we should be confident enough to express all aspects of ourselves.'

She's right. Maureen herself is all those things and fatally disarming with it. As a former air hostess, a model and now a publishing tycoon, she's decided that her contests can help give Indian women the voice that they've been lacking for so long. And at first glance, these aren't the shy retiring wallflowers or harping harridans that stereotypes have suggested. Maureen's asked me to help judge the contest and I have to say, surrounded by all these beautiful women, I have to suppress the inner giggling schoolboy that's threatening to burst out and unmask me.

The youngest contestant is 21 and the eldest we're seeing today is 49. The ladies are expected to have beauty, poise, decorum, a decent general knowledge and a marriage certificate. The judging panel consists of Maureen, myself and two former winners of Mrs India, both of whom have used their winners' status as a platform to get into the media. The contestants nervously move in and out before me like some sort of fabulous sushi conveyor. I subtly check to make sure I'm not drooling.

The questions start rather endearingly: 'What would your in-laws think of you taking part in a swimsuit round?' and 'Did your husband enter your name in the contest?' They then take a completely bizarre

turn: 'What would you do if your husband confessed to being bisexual?' 'Adolf Hitler, was he a good or a bad man?'

When it's my turn to ask the questions I decide to ask one of the more surreal ones on the list: 'You come downstairs one morning to find your husband has turned into a refrigerator, what do you do next?' Although I hid behind my list in embarrassment, the girl, with a glittering tiara in her mind, gamely answered everything that was thrown at her. (Her answer, in case you're curious, was: 'I would open the door and cool myself by him.' You can make up your own minds about that.)

'Right,' says Maureen decisively. 'Next, the swimsuit round.' I get ready my most business-like face and steel myself for the responsibilities looming. After all I'm here to judge not gawp, dammit! As I rather professionally tuck my notes under my arm and make sure the top is on the correct end of the biro, Maureen's manicured hands prevent me from going further. 'No men allowed,' she says, smilingly but firmly. I attempt a half-hearted argument about being a judge, but this is India and there is a strict decorum about such matters. Besides, I'm outnumbered.

In any case, it was a memorable way of spending an afternoon and incredibly revealing, giving us a view of women with power and women with aspirations in twenty-first-century India. India is effectively a matriarchy; from Sonia Gandhi down, it's the women that call

ABOVE: Winners of the Mrs India pageant. Sorry, boys, they're taken. The sign on the right could be describing me, though I refuse to prostrate myself on fruit.

the shots, it's the women that run the families and now, increasingly, it's the women who run big business.

One of them told me, after the audition was over, that if you wanted sausages there was no need to keep a pig in the house. I'm still trying to work out what she meant. But I suspect it doesn't say a great deal for Indian men.

City of nightmares

Friends of mine who've lived in Bombay have expressed the idea that Bombay doesn't really have an identity of its own at all, that more than anything else it wants to be Los Angeles except it lacks the basic infrastructure to make this a reality. I decided to hit the streets the following morning to find out more.

Our hotel was down by the waterfront in Colaba. Most tourists in Bombay arrive here and as a result the streets are thronged with stalls selling 'I'm with Stupid' T-shirts and plastic models of the Taj Mahal. But less than a hundred yards away from the hotel's gleaming façade is the waterfront.

Down here tiny fishing villages have managed to survive despite the modern India that's springing up around them. In the background gleaming towers of steel and glass, the new face of Bombay, dominate the skyline, but down here it's as if things haven't changed in a hundred years.

There are ponies and open dung fires, children wearing threadbare rags, floating on massive bundles of discarded plastic. They're part of Bombay's vast economic underclass. This city is infamous for being home to some of Asia's largest slums and I could see first hand what life for those at the bottom of the pyramid was like: shelter from the rain provided by blue corrugated plastic, brown drinking water, an entirely hand-to-mouth existence.

On my way back to the hotel, I saw some slums being cleared; bulldozers and an army of police wearing brown uniforms that looked

LEFT: Poverty is indiscriminate when it comes to gender and age. The woman that bears such a burden would be collecting her pension in Britain.

for all the world like a team of wasps destroying an ant hill, descended on the makeshift huts and began their process of shouting and waving their arms threateningly. The air was filled with noise, the sound of families screaming for their homes and their possessions and the sound of bulldozers. A bystander told me that this is happening more often as real estate now has a human cost. His friend added that it was a good thing, that these people were there illegally and didn't pay taxes. I didn't have the nerve to point out to him that 20 per cent of nothing was nothing. Nobody seemed to know where these slum dwellers were going. I suspect that the slum dwellers didn't have much idea either.

People were rushing about frantically trying to save a few precious items and pushcarts lined the side of the road. Each cart carried the worldly goods of a family. This was India's city of dreams, as city of nightmares. Progress and modernity may have arrived for some but others are clearly paying the price.

India famously now has a population of over a billion people, and finding out what the future holds for this country is going to take a lot more investigation. Will the rich get richer and the poor get poorer or is there some strange revolution ahead, some great elegant solution that's about to present itself?

CHAPTER TWO

Into the Future

Bangalore is the city that's become synonymous with India's seemingly dominant role in processing the world's data. For the last fifteen years, this South Indian metropolis has become almost a byword for Indian technical excellence. The information-technology boom in India claims this city as its hub. Thirty years ago, this was a pleasant university town with a reputation for having a laid-back and faintly bohemian atmosphere. Wide open spaces and airy boulevards meant that Bangalore was marketed as India's garden city, but three decades of development have hugely affected the city's character – and unfortunately the garden city described in out-dated guidebooks is hardly recognizable.

Once-green spaces have given way to high-rise blocks, and the city's fragile infrastructure has virtually fallen apart under a vast influx of people. Poor sanitation, overcrowding, oversubscribed utilities and shocking roads have all combined to transform short scooter rides into interminable road journeys – and the traffic here is as bad as I've seen anywhere in India.

To understand why this has happened in Bangalore, you have to look a little way back into India's recent past. For forty-odd years after Independence, India hobbled along on a socialist economy left behind by the nation's founding fathers, Mahatma Gandhi and the first Prime Minister, Jawaharlal Nehru.

OPPOSITE: Bangalore traffic. 'Hi honey, I'm a mile from home. See you in about four hours.'

Their grand socialist vision was beautiful but bound to failure; endemically corrupt, enormous and ungovernable, over the course of four decades the Indian government gradually transformed itself from hopeful democracy into bumbling bureaucracy.

Prime Minister Indira Gandhi (Nehru's daughter) took things a step further during her tenure in office by nationalizing all foreign companies, thus shutting out all western investment in India. These policies succeeded in making India self-sufficient in the area of food but forced the country to the brink of bankruptcy in the 1980s.

Then in 1991, the then Finance Minister, Manmohan Singh, put into action a series of economic reforms that would transform the nation. The package was called 'Open Skies' – and India's current economic boom is largely a result of Manmohan Singh's bold policy.

The key to the success of Open Skies was that it would allow multinational companies to invest in India; firms that had been firmly shut out during the socialist era, including Coca-Cola, Nike and Microsoft, could now out-source to India and take advantage of the country's much cheaper labour market.

The country's remarkable transformation was under way, and it rewarded Oxbridge-educated Singh by making him its Prime Minister in 2004. Bangalore was swept along on the economic tidal wave that ensued and if a city exists that embodies the hopes of India's newly created middle classes, Bangalore is widely regarded as being it.

In the 1960s, Bangalore became the site of India's new space programme and the city rapidly established itself as a hub for scientific research and technological innovation.

In addition, rumour has it that all the smart young Indians excelling in IT in Silicon Valley in the USA would chat to their buddies 'back home', which served as an inspiration to the Indian mathematics and engineering geniuses back in the old garden city. 'If Indians could do so well in IT in America, why couldn't the Indians in India do the same?' they asked themselves. Very soon they were providing technical solutions to their brethren thousands of miles away in California.

When India threw its financial doors open to the rest of the world with the Open Skies policy, Bangalore became the first port of call in terms of high-tech investment. A vast complex to the north of the old town was built to serve the New World market. It's called Electronics City, and it's here at the gates of India's Silicon Valley that my rather surreal vision of Bangalore begins.

Having battled for over two hours in heavy traffic, on a journey that I'm told took no more than 45 minutes in the old days on the main arterial road north, I emerge from the crew van slightly frazzled and disorientated. Two immaculately dressed security guards inspect the vehicle and the crew and we apologize for the way we smell. They don't laugh.

We're led into a security cabin, where our pictures are taken for our ID passes.

'You know how the camera puts on ten pounds?' I joke with the inscrutable security-camera-badge-pass wallah.

'No,' he says, not bothering to make eye contact.

People leaving are under as much scrutiny as those entering the building. Industrial espionage is treated with utmost seriousness and data protection is seen as paramount – not just as sound business practice but also to ensure India's commercial reputation remains intact.

An electric golf buggy glides to a halt before me and an attractive young woman named Kavia welcomes me aboard. Within seconds, the chaos of India recedes and we're amongst the manicured lawns of Infosys, one of India's leading data processing centres and the destination for many of the West's leading multinationals' IT needs. Futuristic towers of steel and glass slide past my field of vision. Perhaps most noticeable is the lack of background noise. The campus is a utopian oasis of calm nestled in amongst the usual Indian madness.

Kavia gives me the guided tour of the complex: twenty-four square kilometres of post-modern dreamscape. The architecture is like something out of *Logan's Run*; some of it looks mightily familiar.

'Many of the buildings have been modelled on the founders' favourites from all over the world, see? That one there is based on –'

'The Sydney Opera House,' I interrupt. 'But what hi-tech things are going on in there?'

'It's a food court,' says Kavia. 'In fact there's three that are international cuisine. There's also a gymnasium, a clothing store, a bank and other facilities for the employees.'

So here in suburban Bangalore, a building inspired by the Sydney Opera House sits happily beside a glass Origami tower, and ever-more ambitious structures are sprouting in every direction, including one that just looks like a giant turbine engine.

Imagine the most expensive university in the world and you're close. Then imagine that this university has billions and billions of dollars pouring in every year and is going out to recruit the very brightest graduates available from all over the world, not just India. That's the scale and ambition of Infosys – and it's growing year on year. Last year, Infosys's revenue topped $2 billion.

Our golf cart silently pulls up outside a large blue-glass pyramid modelled on the one beside the Louvre in Paris; it's surrounded by water.

'Our broadcast centre,' Kavia tells me proudly.

Reflected in its surface is something that looks like an enormous satellite dish, 'The Terminal', another one of the many company canteens serving multi-cuisine food. I'm having lunch with a group of young employees. Over burgers and fries complete with Coke, they tell me about how their aspirations have changed from those of their parents.

'We have things our parents couldn't afford at our age, like we have our own cars and can take foreign holidays.'

'How many of you earn more than your fathers ever did?' I ask.

Every single one of them raises a hand.

'How does that make you feel?' I ask.

'Guilty,' they answer quietly in unison nodding their heads. 'We have seen how hard they worked, just to maintain the family home and

BELOW: The futuristic broadcast centre at Infosys, Bangalore. Could I have the room with the window, please?

especially to give us a good education and we've started earning more than them in half the time.'

I suspect that they will be the last generation to feel such humility towards their parents. Their own children, the first generation born in the IT age, will be born into wealth, comfort and privilege. In homage to H.G. Wells, the inmates of the Infosys campus have their own name – they are known as 'Infosians'. Most of this happy little group at lunch are just twenty-four years old. I ask them if they're interested in working abroad, say in Britain or America.

'Not really, we've travelled to these places and seen what they have to offer. We can get everything here that you get there and our money goes further here, and India is a happening place right now, lots of opportunities, even just within our company … also we're with friends and being near to family is really important, so what would we gain from moving abroad? Though it is really nice to take vacations abroad.'

This young group are a great advertisement for modern, globally connected India. They're smart, savvy and have disposable income and, interestingly, they retain those 'family values' that politicians in the West so routinely trot out.

The Infosys campus is a remarkable site in its own right, but it's when you enter the 'GMC' or Global Monitoring Centre that you can see the extent to which India's technological reinvention appears to be without limit. Getting into the GMC building requires special security clearance. In order to get past the automated entry system, one has to go through a space-age device that uses lasers to scan the palm of the right hand. One has to wait for a moment while the machine decides whether you are indeed the person you claim to be. If you're lucky, the indicator light silently turns from red to green, and you're in.

I'm not so lucky; the indicator light stays an imperious red and the heavy glass door resolutely shut. My Infosys guide, Kavia, is my passport in. After she has triple-checked with all sorts of mysterious levels of management, she beckons me over and places her own hand on the palm-print reader.

ABOVE: Another mammoth construction at Infosys. At least the gardens are finished.

OVERLEAF: Bangalore's road infrastructure struggles to keep up with daily demands – it almost falls apart in unexpected weather changes.

47

The prize for having an approved palm-print is entry into a sealed glass room that is home to hundreds of identical computer terminals. And believe me, these are no ordinary computer terminals. From here, you can link into all the major servers and computer networks in the world and from this very room, Infosys's clients' data security is ensured.

Inside the glass enclosure, hundreds of skilled technicians are patched in to the worldwide web and what they're very effectively doing is preventing problems before they happen.

A vast computerized map of the world dominates one wall. When a computer network in Los Angeles or Beijing looks close to reaching its

BELOW: Take an auto rickshaw ride to the bright lights of Brigade Road for night-time shopping and trendy bars. Can I have an olive in my Molotov cocktail?

processing capacity limit, an alarm sounds and hundreds of computer operatives are instantly on the case, making sure that the network in question doesn't crash. These skilled technicians can re-route the information travelling from one computer to another in the same office on the other side of the world if a system overload is imminent.

When one considers just how much of modern life relies on computers to keep going (everything from aeroplanes to hospitals and nuclear weapons), it's sobering to realize just how crucial this room has become. Microsoft and Wall Street are just two of the big names amongst many that rely upon this room to make sure that their computer systems keep running.

Such have been the cost savings and efficiency of Indian-based IT companies that many multinationals such as American Express, British Telecom and British Airways have moved the vast bulk of their data processing here to Bangalore, from e-tickets for flights to reminders of an unpaid bill.

All this foreign money pouring in has created a truly new kind of Indian city in Bangalore. As night falls, the trendiest place to hang out is called Brigade Road. It's a neon blur of shopping malls, bars and

restaurants and here anything you desire can be bought, for a price. Flagship stores that pander to the new middle class's consumption include Levi, Nike and Sony. The young professionals who throng the streets are listening to iPods and chatting into mobile phones, just as they would anywhere else in the developed world.

But lest we forget, this is India, and just a few hundred yards away from the swish designer boutiques and coffee-shops are shacks and shanty towns, where entire lives are lived out under plastic sheeting and corrugated iron.

At first glance, it seems that India's recent economic boom is producing a clash of tectonic proportions, a rapidly widening gulf between the haves and the have-nots. It is convenient for those that support free market economics to point at India's Open Skies policy of attracting international investment as the reason for India's burgeoning commercial success and the dramatic rise in the middle class. However, they shy away from citing those whose front door is a sheet of polythene and back wall is a billion dollar IT business.

Unlike traditional heavy industry, much of the data processing-based industries don't require much ancillary work, hence there's less likelihood of a trickle-down effect in terms of employment. India has always lived with the contradictions of the super-wealthy and the super-poor but this recent economic acceleration could leave half a billion people behind in its wake. This is India's biggest and most severe challenge.

Boom Bangalore?

Another grey morning in Bangalore. Raptors circle low over the city's water coolers. The suburban day is already well under way as I walk the short distance from the hotel to my first appointment. On the streets I pass people selling fruit and vegetables under damp plastic awnings, fragile puddles reflecting the wheels of bicycles and carts. They seem oblivious to the revolution happening around them.

The recent creation of all this new wealth has left young Indian entrepreneurs with a novel dilemma – after all, what can you sell to the person who already has everything? Well, you can sell them something new to aspire to. These days the big money to be made is in selling dreams, and it transpires that the new money has not just rejuvenated existing markets, but created new ones.

Enter Richard Branson and a group of rather wily Indians who have set up a new enterprise to tap into this burgeoning market. The result is Virgin Comics, an Indian company ostensibly selling Indian graphic novels to Indians.

Most of my holidays to India as a child did consist of me badgering various adults to get me comics. In England growing up, I regularly perused *The Beano*, *Whizzer 'n' Chips* or *The Dandy*; these were fine for my tabloid fix. If I wanted to go to the equivalent of a broadsheet, I would turn to *Superman* and *Spiderman*.

However, when I was confined to hot days without telly in Delhi and Karnal, ingesting comics was my only way of remaining sane. *Archie* comics were, for some bizarre reason, the most widely available comic book about. The adventures of Archie and his friends, Jughead, Betty and Reggie, in small-town 1950s and 1960s America seemed to captivate the Indian populace. These comics never found massive success in England, so I thought initially they were Indian, until it dawned on me that there weren't many ginger-haired kids in India.

The only omnipresent superhero comic was 'The Phantom', a slightly odd eye-mask-wearing, gun-toting vigilante who wore a one-piece purple outfit, including cowl. What made him confusing to me was that he rode a horse and all his adventures took place in the jungle. I mean, where did he get his bullets from? Or his designer boots made? And, primarily as a kid from west London trying to find refuge from the heat, why the hell was he wearing a damn cowl … in the jungle?

I gorged myself on these two comic worlds and then came across like an idiot when I tried to explain the characters to kids back in London. Inevitably their first question after hearing me out would be, 'Why is he wearing a cowl … in the jungle?'

I hope Virgin Comics are not going to make me feel like an idiot when I get back to London …

Behind the façade of an otherwise entirely anonymous-looking office building in the suburbs of Bangalore, new superheroes are being created especially for the next generation; not just Indian versions of familiar heroes like Spiderman and the Incredible Hulk, but new characters aimed specifically at the young Indian consumer.

The results are intriguing, and give me a remarkable window on the world of the adolescent male Indian psyche. Incarnations of Hindu

ABOVE: Wild west hero. Hounslow was a frontier type town in the 1960s. I was a cowboy. The rest of the family were Indians.

OPPOSITE: 'The Sadhu', Indian comic hero with pet cat.

deities wield semi-automatic pistols with silencers instead of mythical celestial weapons, women with the power to transform themselves into snakes, hermits who can tell the future. It seems the average reader responds well to stories shot through with elements of traditional mythology, yet with enough sex, violence and technology to appeal to the techno-geek teenager in him.

All these new characters are set against a futuristic, dystopian backdrop reminiscent of Ridley Scott's *Bladerunner*. As in reality, the old and the new coexist with profound mutual indifference in India's dreamscape. Here the minarets of a mosque support a monorail, and hovercars have to negotiate cows and beggars in the street.

The new comics are doing very well, but they're really just a testing ground for those truly industrial dream-factories – the movies. Characters including 'The Sadhu', developed here in Bangalore, have already been exported to Hollywood and have big-name talent attached. Superstar directors including John Woo are working with Virgin Comics to develop ideas from storyboard to silver screen. I pitched my own comic-book extravaganza, but a guy whose special powers were limited to being able to alter the size of his enemy's underwear, despite having a monkey in a hat as a sidekick, met with polite offers of accompanying me out of the door. Even Indian dreams have become worth something these days, it would appear, unless of course they involve a monkey wearing a hat.

When I was a child, whenever we came to India our relatives wanted us to bring them things from England. These items were precious by definition, the very idea of things being imported from the West elevating them from mere objects into status symbols. Every year, I would bid goodbye to a favourite pair of jeans or a baseball cap that one of my cousins had extorted from me.

Today, the world is a different place. The young employees at Infosys have no desire to emigrate; indeed, many of them are choosing to come back to India having studied abroad, giving up American passports for a better life here in Bangalore. My cousins are now sending

me jeans and baseball caps. It's as if a new type of confidence has emerged in India's collective consciousness: a very real sense of self-assuredness in the way that young Indians carry themselves today.

Ever since the Raj, in western literature and film, Indians have been portrayed as meek, passive, industrious creatures reminiscent of the noble savage of Ruskin or Huxley. Certainly in movies and television, the image I had of my own heritage was the same as everyone else's. Apart from the fat unheroic Maharajas, Indians were generally portrayed as mystical vagabonds with exotic pets. An elephant or monkey was the usual shorthand for Indian, with the occasional tiger or cobra thrown in if it was felt the viewer still had some doubt. Normal Indians were generally portrayed as faceless workers who didn't understand the intellectual 'civilized' nature of the West and were bemused by such things as technology.

Of course, I knew all of this to be untrue. I had cousins who worked in agriculture and textile research and were always talking about various breakthroughs that were pending. I knew. My parents knew. The world, however, did not.

Now, it seems, all that is finally changing.

As I write this, India's home-grown space programme is taking leaps and bounds. The country's first re-usable space vehicle has just safely landed in the Bay of Bengal, and an Indian astronaut has just travelled to the International Space Station.

BELOW: The graphic novel goes native. The brilliant artists at Virgin Comics, Bangalore.

The television news is currently dominated by rather surreal images of this impressive young Indian woman, with her hair flowing around her head in zero gravity like a halo. Who'd have believed it ten years ago? A female Indian astronaut giving press conferences to her proud nation, live from space? Today the Indian government has proudly announced its intention to send Indians to the moon within the next decade, and all this astonishing progress has emanated from the research done here in Bangalore.

In the bar of the hotel, that evening, I got talking to a young man called Ash who, inevitably in Bangalore, worked within IT, but in the

far more exciting area of 'military defence' systems. He looked less like the guy who may have designed 'the button' and more like a sci-fi geek. In fact we talked about *Star Trek* for half an hour before I could ask him about India's cutting-edge technologies such as space exploration and, of course, the nuclear issue.

'Well, I suppose from an international point of view, one of the more problematic aspects of this rapid technological development is India's nuclear programme. We've always had the ability to innovate and find our own solutions to technical challenges. There was some technical help from the old Soviet Union, but no technology came through from the West, until recently, but we still managed to develop a successful space and nuclear programme including home-grown nuclear weapons.'

I already knew that the Nuclear Non-Proliferation Treaty limited the possession of nuclear weapons to those who had them before 1967. The treaty, ratified by most countries, went into effect in 1970, and was largely successful in putting the brakes on the nuclear race. Crucially, India, Pakistan and Israel did not sign it.

Ash continued, 'I know many western nations objected to India's nuclear weapons programme, but we perceived threats at that time from Pakistan, which was also developing them and China already had them – what were we supposed to do? Also it was technology we were developing ourselves, our solutions to our problems.'

India's nuclear tests in the deserts of Rajasthan first hit the world headlines more than ten years ago, and they were rapidly responded to by Pakistan's own nuclear missile tests, although India's first atomic test was conducted in 1974.

India, Pakistan, China and North Korea all have or are close to possessing nuclear weapons. Add into the mix the instability of Afghanistan and we have a lot of vying powers in relative proximity. One can only pray that all these terrifying weapons stay as deterrents.

Ash's mates arrive and they move on to discuss *Star Wars* versus *Star Trek* as they saunter off to another trendy Bangalore drinking hole.

CHAPTER THREE

God's Own Country

Turn on the television in India today and a bewildering array of images assaults you. Adverts for cosmetics and sports cars jostle for position with soap operas and pop music. Skin bleaching for both men and women give way to India's biggest movie star telling us that a certain brand of *churan*, a popular herbal digestion powder, 'is necessary'. Over the last fifteen years, the two part-time TV channels that used to monopolize the Indian airwaves have been swept away by the cable, satellite and digital revolution. There are over a dozen English-language channels, plus a plethora of movie, music and news channels. On several occasions I turn on my hotel television set to find my own younger self staring back at me. Freaky. Today, my remote control has more to choose from here in India than it does at home.

One of the striking changes I notice as I casually channel-surf, apart from the number of 'foreign brands' being proffered to the cash-rich young middle class, are the commercials advertising India itself. With landscapes ranging from tropical beaches, sweeping deserts, dense verdant jungles and alpine towns to snow-clad Himalayan retreats, India has always had a lot to offer to the western tourist. However, vacations as we know them have never been part of the Indian culture. When my parents or uncles and aunts spoke of holidays, it meant going to stay with your grandparents for the summer. Or at the very most, going on

OPPOSITE: Taking in the stunning Keralan backwaters. Cool shades, cool hat, cool spare tyre (not the one around my waist!).

a pilgrimage, which meant sleeping on the floor of an ashram, eating basic non-spicy food and dressing in plain white cottons. No finding the nearest disco and getting wasted in the adjoining bar.

India's rich and varied vistas were reserved solely as locations for Bollywood songs, often incorporating all of them within a single number. 'I love you,' would croon the hero, balancing precariously on a glacier. 'I love you,' the heroine would coyly answer back, peeping from around a palm tree. However, as the middle class has embraced more western lifestyles, they have been increasingly keen to live out their Bollywood fantasies by taking their holidays in India itself. My uncle and aunt who, in their first seventy years of life, hadn't been anywhere, have, in the last eight years, been everywhere. They've taken trips to the Himalayas, and ventured down to the sun-kissed beaches of Goa and even across the sea to the Andaman Islands in the Indian Ocean off the coast of Sri Lanka. Their grandchildren, now working for large multi-nationals, have cajoled and inspired them to travel to all those wonderful locations they'd only previously seen in the movies.

One of the most desired holiday destinations has become the state of Kerala on the south-western coast. The young IT professionals of Bangalore and Hyderabad head there to holiday, or even just chill out for a couple of days.

TV ads feature a series of idyllic landscapes, temples, beaches and luxury hotels, complete with scantily clad beautiful women, sipping cocktails beside an azure sea. Visit Kerala, God's Own Country, the commercials urge, palm trees and sunset cruises await. Who am I to resist?

This is India's wild and beautiful Malabar Coast. Even its name has the appropriate nostalgic sonority to it – Malabar, land of spices, home to tea and coffee plantations and dense tropical jungles. Elephants, wild boar, sloth bears and leopards are still found in these forests, and this state, one of the world's 25 top biodiversity hotspots, has to date managed to keep industrial development in check.

My entire family have always raved about this part of India, talking about it with a bizarre misty-eyed kind of reverence, a thousand-yard

ABOVE: Though tourism is booming, Kerala's traditional fishing industry is suffering.

stare that reminds one slightly of how supersized Americans talk about all-you-can-eat buffets.

Kerala, however, is a lot more than the super-duper widescreen, fast-edited intoxicating images pounding my senses. It has an enviable social record. The state tops All-India league tables in public health and social welfare. It is claimed that it has 100 per cent literacy and is so fêted that it's been held up by social scientists around the world as the 'Kerala Model', a shining example of how social development can work in practice. And all this within the first and arguably most enduring democratically elected Marxist government in the world.

It is with a spring in my step that I board the jet to Kochi (the renamed Cochin), commercial capital of Kerala and reputedly one of the most charming cities in southern India. The short flight from Bangalore gives me just enough time to wolf down my vegetable cutlet snack and peruse still further glossy images of my destination in the in-flight

ABOVE: I still go weak at the knees around exotic fruit. I almost fainted when I saw this lot.

OPPOSITE: Surveying the produce at one of Kerrala's many markets.

magazine. As soon as we touch down, the warm sunshine, clean air and swaying palm trees bring a smile to my face. I bring out a cowboy hat that Gautam gave me in Bombay, and I'm as prepared as I can be.

My first impressions on our trip to the hotel is that there is something old world about this place. It seems free of the overpowering bustle that defines so many Indian cities. The air feels fresher and the people seem a lot more laid back. Since it's still early, I decide to take a short ride to the centre of Fort Cochin, 'about a twenty-minute drive' from the main city of Kochi, I'm told at the hotel reception.

For three thousand years traders from around the world sailed to Kerala for its pepper, cardamom and cinnamon. Arguably, it was the desperate race to find a sea route from Europe to Kerala that set western explorers looking for India in the first place, and in 1498 Vasco da Gama secured his place in the history books when he finally landed in Calicut, northern Kerala.

But Kerala's contact with the outside world stretches far further back into the mists of time than the arrival of da Gama and the Portuguese. Scholars date the Jewish community here back to the sixth century BC, and the apostle St Thomas is reputed to have visited this beautiful coastline in search of converts at the very dawn of the Christian faith.

The last remnants of the old European town, founded in the sixteenth century, are still here and are amongst the most romantic of India's many cultural time capsules. In an era of political correctness and unrepressed renaming the area is perhaps surprisingly still called Jew Town.

I walk through the network of narrow streets and find an old synagogue at its heart; it seems strangely exotic to find the Star of David enmeshed within the ironwork of window gratings. Even stranger is to find a sign on the synagogue wall, that tells you to 'Please dress modestly' in English and Hebrew. I stop momentarily, waiting for Woody Allen to appear. He doesn't.

The synagogue itself is extremely simple. Plain whitewashed walls and a clock tower dating back almost two hundred and fifty years. At

dusk, the sinking orange sun illuminates dilapidated Portuguese warehouses in dusty shafts of light. The atmosphere is calm and laid back and I'm surprised that not even the local traders express that rather frenzied happy sales attack I've come to associate with India.

Many of the old spice houses have now been converted into antique shops where the former contents of the town's grand European mansions can be bought at extortionate prices, but aside from the old-world charm of Cochin the real draw of this region lies in its spectacular natural beauty – most famously, a narrow 360-mile chain of rivers, lagoons and lakes wedged between a long mountain

range called The Western Ghats and the Arabian Sea known as the Backwaters.

Because of its proximity to the Arabian Sea, Kerala is the first state each season to receive the monsoon rains, and most of the region's innumerable rivers and backwaters are almost entirely monsoon fed – fluctuating wildly in size from small rivulets in the summer to raging torrents in the rainy season.

By far the best way to see the abundant natural beauty of the area is by boat, and after the congestion of Bombay and Bangalore, I don't take any persuading to board a thatched houseboat. Cruising along and

OVERLEAF: Mahouts and elephants during the spectacular festival of Thrissur Pooram.

65

ABOVE: Though he's smiling, soon this could be his entire day's catch.

OPPOSITE: The stunning Chinese fishing nets, disappearing fast.

breathing in the languid, tropical air feels like joy, relief and lying in a hammock with a good book eating banoffee pie, all rolled into one. This could get dangerously addictive.

From the main channel of Kerala's most important river, the Periyar, I can see hundreds of tiny canals branching out seductively into the rainforest. In a happy daze of adventurousness (and probably because I'm wearing a cowboy hat), I decide to explore one of these.

These are the true Backwaters, a dizzying array of narrow straits which are home to much of Cochin's rural population and they retain the precious, dreamy cocoon of an ancient lifestyle. We lazily float past fishing villages and medieval churches, backyards just inches from the water, washing lines hung with laundry that dries imperceptibly slowly in the warm humid air. Occasionally, a lone boatman bobs past in a vessel so small that he looks as if he's paddling a child's hat. As he gets closer, I realize he is indeed in a boat, but I'm still not convinced that it isn't an origami one made from a sheet of A4.

The lack of heavy industry in this particular stretch of the area (offset by plenty in other parts elsewhere) means that apart from our boat engine putt-putt-putting away gently like a flatulent monk on a vow of silence, we are serenaded by the sounds of nature. Bliss.

At first glance, little has changed here since the days of the great explorers, and one can imagine the narrow barges and long canoes that once plied these canals, piled high with their mouth-watering cargo — kernels of nutmeg and fierce red chillis, vibrant turmeric and fragrant cinnamon.

One sad image that tells no uncertain story, however, is the decayed remains of Chinese fishing nets. Once a thriving part of Kerala's cottage fishing industry, the nets are still used as romantic allure for tourists. But further into the backwaters, they have fallen prey to the definitely unromantic march of 'progress'. As we slowly chug along, the abandoned nets rise up out of the water like the skeletal remains of some dinosaur — the nets long gone, just the structures remain, along with the rotting jetties that once felt the urgent feet of livelihood.

ABOVE: Thatched houseboats on the backwaters allow you to take in Kerala's natural beauty at a leisurely pace.

Today, there is very little in the way of agricultural traffic on the Periyar River. Instead, the most common sights are tourist ferries and impossibly large supertankers making their way to the international container port.

Cochin is, like the rest of India, undergoing a renaissance and as a result the sleepy fishing town is rapidly undergoing dramatic changes.

Gone fishing

I'm staying at the Brunton Boatyard, a luxurious eco-resort perched right on the riverbank. It's been modelled on the Portuguese wharves of old and is very popular with Europeans as an atmospheric, serene

70

getaway where they can have an ayurvedic massage and catch some rays. But all is not well in paradise.

As I have my breakfast by the pool I can see the constant to and fro of enormous dredgers; the Periyar River is being relentlessly deepened to allow for the increasing supertanker traffic, despite the growing protests of scientists who fear the long-term ecological side-effects. As evidenced by the rotting Chinese fishing nets, it is an accepted fact that fish stocks in the Backwaters have already dropped alarmingly. However, as he expertly refills my coffee cup without breaking eye contact, my waiter tells me that there are some working fishing nets a short distance from the hotel. At sunset I walk down to investigate. At high tide, the enormous cantilevered nets rise and fall like the inner workings of an ancient timepiece and their iridescent silk glistens as it catches the evening sun.

Each net is hauled out of the water by a line of fishermen who heave against the weight of the water, a tug-of-war in which the groaning wooden skeleton reluctantly gives way to reveal its meagre burden of silver fish. The waterfront remains a hive of activity, a scene reminiscent of a medieval battlefield – after the battle. I get chatting to one of the owners, a middle-aged man called Vincent, who tells me sadly that these majestic fishing contraptions are now largely a tourist attraction.

'Many of them were passed down from generation to generation, this particular one –' he said, pointing to his own net '– has been in the family for hundreds of years, but it doesn't really make any money.'

'Would you, like so many others have done here, sell it on?' I ask him.

'If I got a good offer I would listen, but who wants to buy a fishing net that doesn't make any profit? And then there's the upkeep, I spent thousands of dollars maintaining it and having new nets made but what for? My children all work in the city so they're not interested.'

I ask Vincent why he still comes down here. 'It's in my blood. These people who work on the nets, they catch fish and they're happy, they don't catch fish, they're happy,' he says.

'So,' I say slightly confused, 'they're happy all the time then?'
'It's in their blood,' responds Vincent conclusively.

I decide to press the matter. 'If the fishing is no longer economically viable, then where can the income come from?'

'Tourists, mainly,' says Vincent, indicating some of the floral-shirted westerners focusing their cameras upon us. 'They will pay in dollars to stand on the nets and have their photos taken.'

Arguably, the adaptable and pragmatic folk of Cochin have found a new way to survive and tourism has provided a vital lifeline, but not all of the Keralan population are thrilled about this fundamental change to their ancient way of life.

'Last year Kerala won an international eco-tourism award and some concerned tourism workers in the state sent a letter to the judges, trying to persuade them not to give Kerala the award,' Vincent tells me.

Over coffee, sitting on the nets as the sun slowly sets, he tells me that their letter of grievance talked of the unsustainable extraction of ground water in tourism hotspots, pollution of the Backwaters caused by tourism, the impact of sex tourism, and poor waste management. 'It has been clearly demonstrated that the claim that tourism as a vehicle for developing the environment in the state is highly questionable at best and unfounded at worst,' it concluded.

All over the world, Kerala has been regarded as a bold social experiment but, like any socialist system, Kerala spends what little resources it has on services such as health care, food and basic education. Critics point to its economic failure and the fact that the 'model state' is effectively propped up by India's national government. The Kerala Model is not without its detractors, but whatever your reservations, you have to admire the stand that the people of Kerala have made against potentially lucrative investment. Financial suicide? Perhaps, but gutsy nonetheless.

One after another, the tiny state government has taken on the world's most influential multinationals, including Pepsi, Coca-Cola and Microsoft, and forced them to justify their capitalist operations in the communist state.

OPPOSITE: 'I think the bra fits perfectly, sir ... er, madam ... er, Goddess Kali?'

RIGHT: Vincent, owner of a fishing net – always happy, despite his struggle to make a living.

On the flipside, the whole neo-Marxist thing can become rather tiresome – especially when one comrade insists you visit another comrade to secure permission to visit a third comrade, who then refers you back to the first. And the state often grinds to a halt while this or that is demanded by the incredibly vocal populace – all of whom seem to sport identical bushy Saddam moustaches.

The cost of rejecting pecuniary advances from multinationals has been to the tourists' advantage. Kerala is one of the fastest-growing tourist destinations in the world, as people flock to the relatively placid pace of life, stunning scenery and clean air, although, as in other parts of India, the infrastructure is at times playing catch up with the development. And, as the constant dredging indicates, how long Kerala can remain an idyll remains to be seen.

It seems a fitting place to end this part of my journey here in Cochin, where India's modern social experiment and ancient history collide.

To remind me of the traditional, at my hotel tonight, there's a performance of Kerala's traditional dance form, Kathakali.

In Kathakali, wildly decorated performers tell India's mythical stories

74

– epic tales of the gods and their battles – through dance. One goddess in particular, Kali, is the subject of tonight's concert. The performers are part dancers, part mime artists, but there seems to be no glamour attached to this part of show business. The artists sit haphazardly on the hotel reception floor, applying their own make-up. They each have their own little box of face paint sticks and each take turns in holding the small shaving mirror while the other perfects their character's look.

I stop momentarily, wondering how ballet dancers in the West would feel, having to sit in such a public place doing something so private. A multitude of traditional instruments – sitars, tablas and south Indian drums – are being tuned and I follow the sounds to the open grassy central veranda of the hotel, where a large pyre is being lit.

The film crew are busily running around holding plugs, barking orders, swearing and falling over things, like a bad comedy warm-up act before the main turn. I take my seat on one of the randomly strewn white plastic garden chairs, the lights dim and the show is ready to begin.

The performance is, predictably, a riot of sound and colour. It revolves around the story of Kali's anger and subsequent wrath leading to the end of the world. The drums, dancers and flames gradually merge, a hypnotic blaze of orange and crimson. The performance ends with applause from the few assembled guests and the main lights come back on. The dancers wearily remove their masks and quietly, without fuss, barely acknowledging the audience, head off to find some space on the reception floor.

My time in Kerala has come to an end and feels all too brief. Cochin, once a buzzing fishing community, has become a truly beautiful tourist destination. It occurs to me that India seems to have an almost limitless ability to absorb and assimilate change – even a Marxist state like Kerala can be democratically elected and flourish within the overpowering rate of technical and economic progress of India itself. Witnessing the dance of Kali seems an appropriate point at which to end this part of my journey and consider the next stop on my voyage around India, the city of Kali – Calcutta.

BELOW: A traditional Keralan clothes-maker.

PART TWO

THE FARTHEST SHORE

CHAPTER FOUR

Oh, Calcutta

The second leg of my journey begins in one of India's most congested and perplexing cities – Calcutta. There's something about the heady cocktail of heat, crowds and abject poverty that gets under my skin, and that's just at the airport. I have to confess that I feel a mounting sense of trepidation as we crawl through slow traffic towards the centre of the 'city of joy'.

But there's no getting away from it. For this part of my journey, which will take me across north-eastern India up into the mountains, a region which holds the enviable reputation of being India's holistic heartland, there's really no other place to start.

Calcutta, where the Ganges meets the sea. Calcutta, slap bang in the middle of the most densely populated region on the planet. Where more than a million people live on the streets, and where your heart can be broken on a daily basis just by opening your eyes and looking around. But I'm getting ahead of myself. Perhaps I should start at the beginning …

The British city of Calcutta sprang up on the banks of the Ganges in the seventeenth century. With its location on the far east coast of India, it made an ideal gateway to the Far Eastern markets of Rangoon, Singapore and beyond, and a few reminders of the city's illustrious past are still part of the landscape. The architecture is far more varied than I'd imagined: modern urban facades, Mughul domes, colonial monoliths

OPPOSITE: Garlands at Calcutta's flower market, sold as religious offerings. Thank goodness this has replaced human sacrifice!

and buildings that look like the French Quarter of New Orleans, which I'm told actually hark back to the once substantial Armenian community that lived in the city.

My journey into the city proper begins as I cross one of its most distinctive landmarks, Howrah Bridge. Now renamed after Calcutta's most famous son – poet and Nobel laureate Rabindranath Tagore – the bridge was initially commissioned in 1874, alongside the port that had been established in 1870. As a result of flourishing trade thanks to the sheer volume of merchandise passing through the port, Howrah Bridge became invested with huge commercial importance.

With a central span of 1500 feet, Howrah Bridge is still considered an engineering masterpiece, but for me the real magic of this bridge lies in its human cargo. An hour spent on the pedestrian platform is an exercise in people-watching that makes the brain hurt; where impossible loads are hefted through sheer determination alone but without a whimper of complaint.

Since the early twentieth century the bridge has shown signs of distress due to the huge amount of traffic that traverses it each hour, and this is still one of the busiest bridges in the world. An estimated 100,000 cars pass over it daily, along with countless pedestrians, bullock carts, hand-pulled rickshaws and every other conceivable mode of transport besides.

In any case, Calcutta, first 'discovered' by the British in 1690, was gradually transformed into one of the most important shipping hubs in the world. By 1772 it had grown to become the capital of the British

80

Empire in the East, and the city bears the indelible imprint of the Raj at every turn. In places it's like travelling through a dilapidated, tropical version of Victorian London. The dominating edifice that is the Victoria Memorial appears to have fallen fully formed from its true home in South Kensington.

ABOVE: Pony and trap in front of the Victoria Memorial. Despite the British leaving, the respected monument (above right) remains untarnished.

On the Maidan, Calcutta's version of Hyde Park, I met journalist Shubir Bhaumik, a long-time resident of this city of extremes and contradictions. As the sun fell behind the Victoria Memorial, I allowed myself a rather pleasant and rather romantic daydream of Empire, sitting on the lawn, sipping lemon masala tea, a speciality of these parts.

'We Bengalis think of Calcutta as being a city with a soul. Yes, it is poor. Yes, it is crowded. But as a result you are never alone here. If you are in trouble, people will help, whether you have money or not. It is not like Bombay, where with enough money you can do anything you like. This a city with a very, very strong sense of community.'

He tells me that the Maidan is referred to locally as the 'lungs of Calcutta'. I glance around at the rather parched grass and sparse number of trees and stifle my concern. There are no other large open spaces in the city, and with the dust and pollution the pressure on these 'lungs' must be almost insurmountable.

Calcuttans will proudly tell you that this has always been regarded as the intellectual and cultural capital of the country, home to India's national poet Sir Rabindranath Tagore, awarded the Nobel Prize for Literature in 1913, the highly respected film maker Satyajit Ray and the country's largest museum, which boasts over a million exhibits.

81

Selling confectioneries in Calcutta. The kind of food and presentation my parents' friends hankered for back in the early 1960s.

Sitting out there on the vitiligo-like lawn in the early evening sun, it was easy to see Shubir's point about community. Couples walk hand in hand. Numerous groups of children are playing cricket. A pony and trap clops past, brightly decorated with a trail of glinting tinsel. A tram, looking as old as the city, snakes around the outside of the park. As I sip my spicy citric beverage, I spot a guy walking past with a table on his head, chatting casually to his friend, who has a chair on his head. No one bats an eyelid. More than any of the other Indian cities I've visited so far, this part of Calcutta has an easy, relaxed manner about it, despite the chaos lurking just around the corner.

What I didn't realize was that at that very moment, thanks to that steaming cup of lemon tea, I was ingesting something truly horrible – a malevolent virus had already started working its way through my bloodstream and would soon be trying to force itself out every orifice. Retiring to the sanctity of my hotel room I awaited the arrival of Barnes-Wallace's bouncing bomb, and the dam to inevitably be burst.

82

I managed for the only time on my travels to hook up with my family via webcam. My wife and kids appeared like old-fashioned police photo-fit pictures, and the slightest movement turned them into a Picasso-style jigsaw. The accompanying nausea, combined with a tsunami of emotion about missing them all, made me urgently bid them well and retreat to the bathroom. My insides now felt like they were being put through a mangle by a clumsy launderer on steroids. All part of the experience I thought through clenched temples.

I can deal with being ill; I've done it loads of times. I can deal with being away; travel and my innate curiosity about people and places manages to fill the emotional hole left by not having your loved ones about you. However, combine being ill with being away and I become an utterly inconsolable three-year-old. I decide to make myself feel even worse by listening to requiems on my iPod and watching grainy images of those I love on my mobile phone.

But tomorrow is another day and it duly arrives as ordered and on time. After a tentative breakfast, I venture forth into the sensory pressure cooker that is the city.

While the British painstakingly re-created London's splendid houses and churches, the original citizens of Calcutta lived in *bustees* (shanty-towns) along the banks of what's locally known as the Hooghly River. These *bustees* still exist, and Calcutta has often been lamented for the terribly low standards of living endured by the majority of its population. Areas such as Sudder Street are defined by the persistent beggars, who follow tourists like emaciated vultures, and yet Calcutta's tourism board claims that today life for the city's people is better than ever before.

It was the dawn of Indian Independence in 1947 that sealed Calcutta's fate – the region of Bengal was partitioned (like Punjab in the west) into an Indian mainly Hindu west and a Pakistan mainly Muslim east (East Pakistan), and overnight Calcutta became home to thousands of refugees who had fled their homes in East Pakistan (now Bangladesh); by 1951 less than a third of the city's inhabitants had been born here. The floodgates opened again with the India–Pakistan war of

1971 and the creation of India's new neighbour Bangladesh. If this influx wasn't enough, in 1971 the population growth rate soared to nearly 40 per cent.

Calcutta's desperate economic situation has been blamed both on overcrowding and on the Communist Party of India who have dominated politics in the city for more than thirty years. *Bandhs* (strikes) still happen regularly, workers protesting against most policies put forward by the central government in Delhi, and the city often grinds to a halt.

Bengalis have always been politically volatile. Even during the height of the Raj, Calcutta's nationalists were steadfastly campaigning for India's freedom from Britain's colonial clutches. A perplexed Lord Curzon, Viceroy of India, attempted to stabilize the region by splitting Bengal in two in 1905, but the strategy backfired, and instead Calcutta became the hotspot for the Indian Independence movement.

This hotbed of insurgency was clearly no longer an appropriate city for the Imperial capital, and in 1931 New Delhi became the new capital of British India. With the country beginning to pull itself apart from coast to coast, Calcutta's star began to wane and its fine Victorian institutions began to crumble.

Since Independence in 1947, India has been slowly ridding herself of the reminders of British rule, and in 2001 the government of the state of West Bengal officially renamed Calcutta. Henceforth, it would be called 'Kolkata' – closer to an even older local name 'Kalikata': city of the Goddess Kali.

Street names associated with the Raj have also been changed. The old Circular Road has been renamed Acharya Jagadish Chandra Bose Road (or J. C. Bose Road if you're in a real hurry); Harrison Road has become Mahatma Gandhi Road; and Harrington Street has, inexplicably, become Ho Chi Minh Sarani. It reminds one slightly of 1970s' Britain, where student unions in universities across the land suddenly sprouted a Nelson Mandela Bar, a Steve Biko Swimming Pool and Che Guevara Bike Sheds.

84

In reality, like so much in India, it's only on the surface that anything has actually changed. Yes, maps now bear the new nationalist road names and Kolkata is the official title of the city; but the people who live here call it Calcutta, taxis still go by the old names and, as far as I'm concerned, the simplest thing to do is to use the same names that the city residents use. I take a taxi ride around central Calcutta just to get a feel of the place. We drive past some of the few imposing Victorian residences left that sit opposite the Maidan. They look like decrepit dowagers forlornly eyeing the world without their spectacles.

We take a right turn towards the river and I notice for the first time something slightly odd about my driver. He appears to have no left arm. I mentally squirm, not knowing quite how to confirm my fleeting observation. I put it down to a trick of the light or perhaps the after-effects of that bloody masala lemon hemlock I had the day before but then we get to a roundabout. His right arm begins to rotate like a can can dancer's leg and the shirt sleeve of his left arm, flaps ominously to its own tune.

He notices my rather unsubtle, furrowed stare. 'I lost my arm in the '71 war,' he tells me. 'Oh you lost your arm? I can't say I noticed,' I reply like a confused idiot. 'But,' he adds indifferently, 'you get used to it.' He might, but I'm not altogether sure I will as we weave through Calcutta traffic. We drive as close as we can to the river.

It appears that despite dramatic changes, the rise and fall of an empire or two and the dominion of countless governments, Calcutta remains essentially a city built around the river at its heart. This is the very end of the Ganges Delta, where the mighty Ganges breaks up into countless tributaries and joins the sea.

It's worth bearing in mind that for India's 800 million Hindus, this is much more than just a body of water – this is the mouth of the Ganges, the holiest river in the world. For them, this water can expiate your sins, cure all ills and provide a gateway to the next world. It is, itself, divine.

Hinduism is regarded by many as a philosophy rather than a religion, due to its lack of stringent rules. The belief in reincarnation and the focus on the journey of the soul means that the reason to be good and pious during your tenure on this Earth is to move your soul to a higher level of enlightenment for your own good in the next life. Unlike many other religions, there is no reward of heaven or punishment of hell that awaits; there is simply consequence.

The easiest way to understand Hinduism as a belief system with its multiple deities is first to debunk the popular myth that Hindus believe in lots of Gods. In fact Hindus believe in one supreme being, but every aspect of that one God is personified, identified and made distinct. Some of the personifications are part based on animals, most famously Ganesh, who has a human body and an elephant's head. Ganesh is regarded as the 'remover of obstacles' aspect of God. He's also the deity that represents creativity, so has always played a big part in my life.

Apart from the inherent child-like appeal of a deity that looks like a friendly Disney character, I've felt a protectiveness for Ganesh ever since my schooldays, when a teacher smirked in class, 'Sanjeev, why don't you tell us about your animal Gods? There's an elephant one isn't there? Is there a hamster God as well?' Though I was outraged, I was too young to come up with a swift reply. I simply tried to explain Hinduism to her, which was a little ambitious for a thirteen-year-old. Mind you, a year later, when she said, 'Sanjeev, what is it that makes Asians smell so funny?' I had the nerve to say, 'Oh it's something you would be unfamiliar with Miss, it's called soap.' One of the best detentions I ever got.

For Hindus, God is effectively in every living thing, in every drop of the Ganges and every molecule of the atmosphere. For them, Divinity pervades everything and can be seen in daily life – if you only know where (and how) to look.

Philosophers might choose to call it animism or pantheism; the Indians chose Hinduism. In any case, this sort of all-pervasive belief certainly has a fundamental influence on life for this country's billion people.

I ask my one-armed driver about Calcutta's link with Hinduism, when we hit a relatively straight bit of road.

BELOW: The goddess Kali's terrifying form with her necklace of skulls was designed to strike fear into the hearts of her enemies.

'Calcutta is named after one of Hinduism's most important deities, Kali, she is destruction, but from destruction comes rebirth.'

All the images of Kali I've seen, portray her a fearsome, dark, four-armed destroyer, fiery eyes and lolling tongue, a far cry from most of the pantheon of deities with their beatific smiles and meditative eyes. 'If it's about rebirth, then why such a scary image?' I asked my driver.

'With two hands she is destroying, which means that evil will be annihilated, but with the other two hands she is blessing, which means she will also protect the good. The scary expression is that she can terrify and is darker than the most dark evil … also we're living in Kalyug – the age of Kali, where destruction takes place and rebirth will follow.'

Phew! It is one of the joys of Calcutta that in the most unexpected situation you can find a literate, bright, armchair philosopher and here in this clanking cab, where the windows don't work and the driver has one arm, I found mine. The road by the river becomes too crowded for us to advance and I alight from the taxi, giving my driver the biggest tip I've ever given, though I'm embarrassed to say I tried handing over the

ABOVE: 'Indian Idol'. Immersing Hindu deities is seen as part of the cleansing process. Nature's elements were brought together to create the figurine and letting it go in the holy waters, where it will disintegrate slowly and return to the elements, is seen to mirror the human journey.

87

ABOVE: The Garland District, Calcutta.

OPPOSITE: A young boy makes an offering of a lotus flower in Calcutta's sacred river.

tip and shaking hands with him at the same time. My biggest regret is that I didn't even ask his name.

It's an unsettling image, but as I walk down by the riverbank, the busts of garlanded effigies of Kali are a common sight, washing up on the silty shore in drifts before being recycled or cremated. Indeed demand for these effigies is so great that an entire village of potters works year-round to supply figures of astonishing intricacy, which are then ceremonially discarded – an act which, in India, makes perfect sense. In the Hindu cosmic cycle, creation is always followed by growth then decay and destruction – and in this city, every stage of the cycle is visible simultaneously.

According to ancient tribal belief, Kali was a dark destroyer who could only be appeased by human sacrifice. Today, given the anti-social nature of human sacrifice, it seems to have been agreed that flowers and plaster idols will do. The Ganges, given its role as spiritual conduit to the mother Goddess, is the recipient of thousands of offerings daily, and after any major festival countless idols are ritually consigned to the water.

I take one last look at the floating busts, looking like a scene from the D-Day landings and head back towards the hotel.

The rainbow project

Calcutta has had a bad press in the past – the horror and the poverty have turned many compassionate stomachs, inspired countless Hollywood tearjerkers and labelled the city a hopeless loss.

Its twelve million inhabitants contribute to a national monologue so vast and full of contradictions as to be almost unbearable, incomprehensible. One sees the rapid construction of concrete and glass towers and internet cafes with the spectre of death hanging over the poor and disenfranchised right outside; people sipping their café lattes whilst texting on their latest mobile handset, while a mother and child beg for a few pennies. There's no doubt about it; this is a country that

breaks your heart in a new way every day, fractures you in ways that you didn't even realize you could be broken. Almost as if the Fates, despatched from the West on a one-way ticket of free will, came east and set to work on their *magnum opus*.

At least, that's how it appears in one's lowest moments, when the sight of another beggar or street dweller pushes one towards the edge of despair.

But, if you have the staying power, the low moments pass, and in Calcutta more than anywhere else, hope springs eternal, and life triumphs over seemingly insurmountable odds. One figure who became synonymous with the struggle to alleviate poverty was Mother Teresa, and one of her greatest surviving legacies is visible near the city's Sealdah train station.

Countless narrow streets have sprung up around the terminus, an area that is rife with crime, drugs and prostitution. It's into this world that many of the city's children are born, and the number of children living in makeshift dwellings on the streets of Calcutta is estimated to be 100,000, although the true number may be much higher.

In India, every dark monsoon cloud has a shiny silver-plated lining, and Mother Teresa's Loreto Convent is a perfect example – an elite girls' school that teaches in the English medium. Here the people of the city have taken the future into their own hands. While the school produces highly educated women who will go on to play a huge role in the new Indian dream of prosperity and international recognition, it also attempts to alter the very social fabric of the city that surrounds it.

The Principal, a remarkable Irish sister named Cyril Mooney, founded the programme in 1985 and today the school has 1400 children, half of them from wealthy families who pay fees, and the other half from very underprivileged homes who do not. After morning assembly, Sister Cyril introduces me to a volunteer named Sangeeta who gives me the guided tour.

As we walk through the convent's courtyard, I can hear the happy chatter of a thousand children far above me. Over three floors, ordinary classrooms have lessons in progress, but on the top floor of the build-ing a special space is devoted to the Rainbow Project.

Here, the city's street children are brought into the school and taught basic maths, reading and writing skills – the kinds of things that at home we take for granted. The genius of the scheme is that regular pupils from the school (and not teachers) teach the street chil-dren on a one-on-one basis, gradually enabling them to join in with the regular classes. It means that for many of the street children, understandably wary of adults, their anxieties are assuaged by being helped by one of their peers. So I am moved to see nine-year-olds teaching seven-year-olds basic maths and thirteen-year-olds teaching ten-year-olds the English alphabet. I ask the thirteen-year-old English teacher what she would like to do when she's older. 'Be a physicist' comes the rather startling reply. 'Why a physicist?' I ask her. 'Because with that I could go into engineering and then help build things that will help the community.' I remember what I wanted to do when I was thirteen … become a superhero, though I keep it to myself.

The joy of this system is that the poor get an education, and the older, wealthier kids learn about taking responsibility for the poor – an entirely altruistic and beautiful thing. As I spend the morning playing with the kids and going through their English spelling homework with them, it's impossible not to think of my own children and their peer group at home and marvel at how education here is treated with such reverence and respect. In India, children are desperately proud to wear a school uniform and revere their books like holy artefacts, under-standing that these emblems may be the route to a more satisfying life. This is at odds with many western kids, who regard the school uniform as a social straitjacket and books as something to be defaced and derided. Sangeeta tells me:

'During the holidays, some of the older children, after experienc-ing the teaching process here, will go and knock on the door of a house where they've heard there is a poor child and just ask to spend an hour with them, just to talk or even to teach some basics to them.'

ABOVE: The slum kids that the compassionate youngsters of Loreto Convent aim to reach.

I can't help thinking that the gap between western kids' attitudes and this lot here is widening even further, especially in terms of appreciating social responsibility.

It's time for me to go but as I am saying my farewells to children and staff, I notice an especially young girl, perhaps no more than three years old, playing near two slightly older girls. The older girls are in the middle of a lesson but occasionally turn to wipe the little'un's mouth or hand her a toy. I ask Sangeeta about the toddler, as she is by far the youngest person there.

'The three girls are sisters; they were brought in when the youngest was only eighteen months old. There was no word about the parents. Her sisters were four and seven years old at that time but from the moment they came in, they've consistently looked out for their youngest sister, making sure she has eaten, been dressed and is looked after.'

As I'm relating this to the camera a few moments later, I well up and find it difficult to complete my thoughts. The two older girls, not long after being toddlers themselves, and without being told to, have instinctively and innocently expressed compassion of the purest kind. I feel overwhelmed and humbled before this profound rendition of the human spirit.

Everyday the Rainbow Project children hand out food packages to the homeless around Sealdah station (there is a large concentration of the elderly as well as children around this area), the rescued doing their bit to help others. Loreto also runs 'TOT' – a teacher training programme for the female victims of forced prostitution and trafficking. There are now two hundred street children living on the site, and the convent is a vital lifeline.

Although Loreto offers help to many, the programme is but one lifeboat in a sea of destitution. A third of Calcutta's population still live in slums, and it is estimated that half of all Indians live on or below the poverty line. (In sheer numbers, let us not forget that that is around half a billion people.) Even if life in Calcutta has improved, there is still a long way to go.

OPPOSITE: A purveyor of Godly things. The image of Mother Teresa (to the right) is a common sight in Calcutta.

93

Festival of light

We have arrived in Calcutta at an extraordinary time of year and one that children look especially forward to – Diwali – the Hindu New Year.

This is one of the most important Hindu festivals, as well as the most popular, and is celebrated for five continuous days. It's thought of as a time to celebrate the triumph of good over evil, and hope over darkness.

'Diwali' derives from the Sanskrit word 'Deepavali'. This literally means the Festival of Light, and a walk through any Indian city, town or village on the night of Diwali will testify to how seriously the people take it. Every available lamp and candle is lit, and the rooftops are a riot of noise and colour as fireworks light up the night sky.

Diwali honours Lakshmi, Goddess of wealth, beauty and prosperity, both material and spiritual. Hindus associate Lakshmi with good fortune and so paying homage to her ensures success for the coming year. As well as the usual rituals and prayers, homes are made as bright as possible to venerate the Goddess.

Candles and *diyas* (little clay lamps) are often out done by fireworks, electrical displays and neon colours. *Kandils* (bright paper lanterns) are an integral part of Diwali decorations and colourful traditional motifs adorn doorways and courtyards, welcoming Lakshmi into their homes. To indicate her long-awaited arrival, small footprints are often drawn with rice flour and vermilion powder all over the houses. It is believed she visits the brightest, cleanest home first.

My Diwali experience begins at dusk on a suburban rooftop. A hundred families who each live in the neighbouring blocks have come together for their community celebration.

Rockets, roman candles, catherine wheels and fireworks that behave like rudimentary flamethrowers are all lit and tossed haphazardly. Men, women and children all jostle to light the touchpaper. There's no organized display here; indeed there's no organization whatsoever. Although I've always loved fireworks, I can't help watching through narrow eyes

PREVIOUS PAGE:
Diwali Festival of Light. Oil lamps are an integral part of Diwali celebrations. My family in England still use them.

and eyebrows so furrowed that I probably resemble a gargoyle. The proximity of the people to the fireworks themselves is one worry as at times you can't tell them apart, and I'm sure those beautiful, undulating silk saris aren't fire resistant. Nevertheless, the collective bravado carries the day and the young children dance, point and laugh with delight. Multicoloured sparks blaze against the night sky.

Though all Hindus see Diwali as a celebration of happiness and prosperity, different regions attribute different legends to the origin of this very important festival, and for Bengalis, the Diwali celebrations are devoted to the dark Goddess Kali. On every street corner, a temporary temple to Kali is erected by the local residents and on the night of Diwali the streets are thronged with her worshippers.

I make my way through the maze of interconnecting alleys towards the river, occasionally jumping at the sound of a firecracker which has been lobbed in my general direction. I can now hear lots of raised voices: instructions being hollered, occasional whistles being blown, and chanting. It's all in an unfamiliar language, so it begins to wash over me like white noise. As I push on towards the waterfront, the congestion and noise gradually increase until I am part of a swirling mass of humanity, a wave pushing ever forwards towards the holy river.

Down at the water's edge police officers in crisp white uniforms and helmets (looking like misplaced members of the Village People) are attempting to corral the worshippers into an orderly line. But for the most part the collective fervour is too intense for containment, and the crowd has a will of its own. To the water, the group edges further and further, until we are all standing ankle deep in mud.

One after another, vehicles ranging from large trucks to scooters arrive, each bearing an effigy of Kali, with accompanying drummers. Small family idols to deities the size of a caravan are hoisted on to the shoulders of the faithful and ceremonially consigned to the holy river. The regular Calcuttans are suddenly pushed to one side by the police rediscovering their authoritarian zeal as the local MP and then a police chief also dutifully accompany their offerings down to the river's edge, each constable thinking about a possible promotion no doubt.

Then an utterly surreal moment; a cop, probably no more than five feet four, pushes past me and Patrick, our sound man on this trip, and stands staring up at six-foot-plus Jonathon, our camera whiz.

'Hello,' he says finally, and Jonathon manages a friendly but surprised hello back.

'You do a lot of exercise isn't it?' he adds. Jonathon smiles, unsure as to where this is leading.

'You're a very handsome man,' says the cop. 'Very athletic body isn't it?'

Quite frankly, we're enjoying Jonathon's extreme discomfort at this point. Though I'm pretty certain this wasn't a 'pick-up', or indeed a cryptic cultural aspect of the celebrations, it certainly added to my enjoyment of the proceedings. A cacophony distracts the cop and he goes back to shouting duty and we determine to taunt Jonathon for the rest of his life.

The dignitaries depart and normal pandemonium is resumed. Over and over again, the face of Kali slowly disappears into the night-dark water. Tonight, the Ganges has become the graveyard of the idols.

It seems somehow appropriate that today, as India reinvents itself as a nuclear and economic superpower, Kali is believed to be at the wheel. And given the intensity of my first trip to Calcutta, it's also fitting that she rules supreme in this city of extremes and contradictions.

The city serves as an exemplar par excellence of a peculiar phenomenon that you come across again and again while travelling in India – I call it Indian Logic. It's the ability to hold two entirely contradictory beliefs at the same time. For instance, in Calcutta rick-shaw pullers can be seen on every street corner – and nowhere else in India is this such a common sight. But is it really OK for one human being to be pulled along on a cart by another human being with bare feet?

It's a complicated question because now these people's business has been banned. Liberal politicians see it as inhumane exploitation of the poor by the rich – and their solution is to make each and every one of those poor people unemployed.

The ban is now in full force, and these men will need to find a new trade or starve. It's almost as if in an India which is desperate to appear modern and highly developed, these men are now redundant, and it seems the last remnants of a colonial lifestyle are gradually fading away. However, there has been no whole-scale programme to find these people alternative employment. Even in a Communist-run state such as this, socialist ideals don't always reach those that most need it.

This is not a city to travel through inertly like a ghost – it is too heart-breaking, loud and relentless for that – although within the constant Brownian motion of hardship, one can find inspiration and sincere comradeship. But it's time for me to move on. Tonight I'm catching the night train, north, into the tranquillity of the mountains.

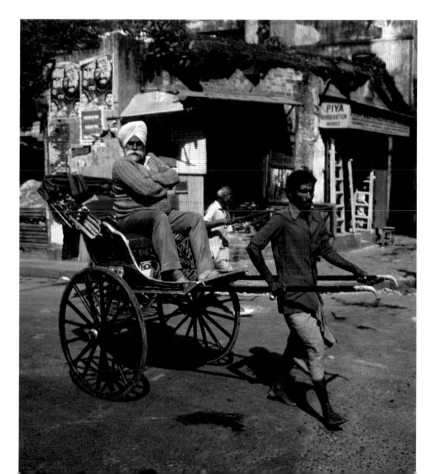

LEFT: Rickshaw puller in Calcutta. The passenger seems determined not to exhale, making it even more difficult to pull him.

CHAPTER FIVE

The Roof of the World

It is with a sense of great relief that I gaze up towards the departures board at Calcutta's Sealdah Station. Every few seconds a loud bong sounds, and the tannoy blurts out another tinny announcement. This is singularly unhelpful as I can't distinguish between the announcements in English, Hindi and Bengali. It's as if I'm being given vital travel information by the teacher in the 'Peanuts' cartoon.

I work my way steadily through the crowds of commuters. A newly arrived railway carriage gushes people like a punctured blood vessel, and where I'm standing at the platform's end, I'm in danger of being swept away by the human tide. I join the eight million other people at the arrivals and departures board, staring up like they're waiting for the mother ship to land in *Close Encounters*.

The next part of my journey will take me north towards the mountains of Sikkim. This will be my first contact with a region of India that has always intrigued me, and will also allow me my first glimpse of the eastern Himalayas.

My destination is Darjeeling, built more than seven thousand feet up on a west-facing mountain slope. The area is a combination of lush tea plantations and breath-taking Himalayan scenery and my journey,

OPPOSITE: Tea estate, Darjeeling. Cuppa, anyone?

beginning with a night train that winds its way steadily uphill, will take in a complicated series of interconnecting roads and mountain passes.

The frail evening light gives way to the fluorescent illumination of the platform – here and there weary travellers with enormous bundles are bedding down for the night. A tea seller trudges endlessly up and down, balancing glass tumblers and an enormous steaming teapot on his shoulders. How come his head doesn't get hot? His nasal chant of 'Chai! Chai! Chai!' becomes hypnotic, meaningless, like the letters of a word that one has stared at for too long. The fluorescent strip lights attract moths the size of bi-planes and I swipe at them like King Kong on the Empire State Building.

A pair of headlights approach from far, far away at the platform's end, and promise the arrival of our train north. Sure enough, a distant horn blares and suddenly the sleepy platform springs into life. Porters wrestle me for my bag, and I willingly give in. My name is printed on a piece of computer paper that has been pinned to the side of the carriage – 'First Class AC Sleeper', the golden lettering above the door proudly proclaims. A small dark stranger smelling of aniseed materializes next to me and insists that he is Sanjeev Bhaskar and announces his intention of boarding my carriage. I tell him that I am Sanjeev Bhaskar and produce my passport victoriously. Without missing a beat, he insists that I am Sanjeev Bhaskar and then, pointing at the manifest, that he is Mr Simon Niblett, who just happens to be our cameraman on this journey. I point out tall fair-haired Simon to him, who may smell of many things, but aniseed is not one of them. The small dark man turns on his heel and confidently marches to the next carriage, where I see him arguing with an official, trying to convince him that he is Mrs Sushila Roy.

We settle into our carriage. The crew and I share a compartment with fold-down bunks, and as night falls the Darjeeling Mail noisily gets ready for bed. Night trains, thanks to the likes of John Coltrane, James Bond and Alfred Hitchcock, have a rather romantic image. This is where spies traditionally battle baddies on hurtling rooftops, where beautiful girls sip gin and tonics in the restaurant car to the strains of soft jazz.

The reality is, unfortunately, rather more mundane. Our 'first class' sleeper is basic, to be charitable; there's no restaurant car and none of the crew look remotely like Jane Seymour. Just as well really, as we have a twelve-hour journey ahead of us. I put on my headphones and try to sleep; the sounds of Lennon and McCartney gradually becomes one with the endless rumble of our wheels on the tracks. I recline in this blissful state for almost ten minutes before we make the first of what feels like a thousand stops. This is the mail train and every postcard, letter and package must be delivered as close to 'on time' as India can allow. I'm an insomniac even when surrounded by every nocturnal luxury that Man has ever conceived, so a clunking train, a quarter of a mile long, stopping every half hour is not best designed with me in mind. Oh boy, those mountains had better be worth it!

Darjeeling has become known around the world for a single reason: tea. For those in the know Darjeeling's crop is said to be the 'Champagne of Tea', produced by combining exactly the right mixtures of soil, sunshine, rain and altitude — and yet its very existence is the result of nature, rather than nurture.

ABOVE: Dawn view of the Himalayan mountain range with part of Darjeeling town in the foreground.

China and Assam tea seeds were first brought by the British to Darjeeling in the 1840s; before this the locals were drinking a black tea imported from Tibet, thousands of miles away. The British combined their love of tea with shrewd colonial ambition, and were trying to break the virtual Chinese monopoly in tea production.

It was an inspired agricultural punt. In 1847, the government distributed 725 kg of tea seeds to the natives of the hills around the area and the first tea gardens were planted. They hoped that Darjeeling's unique micro-climate could out-produce China – and they were right. Tea soon became Darjeeling's only industry and played a major part in the growth both of its population and economy, as well as being a benefit to the whole country.

Today Darjeeling has 86 tea gardens, which produce between 8 and 10 million kilos of tea annually. But this is no ordinary tea. The market for Darjeeling is mainly export, with what has become a world-renowned brand bringing in mainly wealthy foreign buyers. Today Germany and Japan are Darjeeling's largest markets.

I'm heading for Makaibari, the very first of the British tea gardens and one that is using rather unexpected methods to produce, arguably, the world's finest brew. As the sun rises, we pull into Siliguri station and switch from rail to road. Despite total exhaustion after the night's rock and rolling, I now find myself preparing for the three-hour road trip to Darjeeling town.

As we ascend the unexpectedly benign mountain road, my eyes relax and the inertia lifts, as I catch sight of the deepening lush valley and the mist circling the mountain like a ballerina's tutu. The memory of the train clanking its way for half a day, in the manner of a bunch of kids playing home-made percussion for the first time on a sugar rush, begins to fade. I experience a serenity that only nature can bring. Goodbye Calcutta. Hello, Mountains. Now, where's that cup of tea?

Ever since the Industrial Revolution, tea planters have been under the familiar and constant economic pressure of commercial farming: to increase yields and maximize profits. But at Makaibari, a very different ethos is at work – this is a 'biodynamic' plantation, one in which ancient spiritual techniques are being used to cultivate the land, and before you dismiss the whole thing as reading tea leaves, you should bear in mind that these divinely inspired methods have produced the most expensive tea in the world.

For 150 years, the gardens of Makaibari have been in the same family, and the current custodian, Rajah Bannerjee, is one of the most interesting characters in these highlands. His 1500 acres of green tea plantations is situated in Kurseong district, which means 'the land of the white orchid'.

Rajah arrives to meet us on horseback. He looks like a rather distinguished forest ranger, with a genuine Gurkha's hat and khaki uniform. When he speaks, it is with a very clear British inflection – a charming sort of upper-class mumble – and he would not be out of place in a Soho gentlemen's club.

'Hello Sanjeev, welcome to my little patch of paradise.' He welcomes me effusively.

It's difficult to say how old he is – the clean mountain air and healthy living clearly suit him well. His day begins by surveying the gardens and overseeing the different stages of cultivation, and he's kindly invited me along for the ride.

BELOW: Surreptitiously breaking wind in the Makaibari tea gardens (left). The cool Rajah Bannerjee, somehow catching me at it (right).

PREVIOUS PAGE:

Farm workers picking
tea leaves.

As we amble down one of the steep paths, I notice how stunning the scenery is. The lush hills cascade down into the trough of the valley and way in the distance I can see a waterfall, high up seemingly pouring out of the rock face. It suddenly strikes me that I can't hear the waterfall, which indicates its distance and, in turn, its sheer size.

Rajah has a lust for life that is incredibly infectious.

'Sanjeev, have you noticed the wildlife here? Look at the number of dragon flies and butterflies.'

He's right; a quite tremendous number of colourful little insects are flitting happily in their immense playground. I've never seen anything like it, outside trips to botanical gardens.

'It means there's a healthy eco-system here and look here – ' Rajah bounds over to a clump of … well, green stuff, not grass and not weeds, but … green stuff, and lifts it up out of the soil, revealing its roots. 'Come, come, just smell that!' He commands rather delightfully.

It smells of earth, bit peaty, but certainly fresh and certainly not unpleasant, but I'm not really sure what I should be looking for.

'Doesn't smell bitter, does it? There's no smell of mould is there,' says the mountain man.

'No it doesn't,' I agree.

'The soil is so full of nutrients, that the roots remain healthy for ages. This stuff – ' he says, indicating the roots ' – you can actually eat … but I'm not going to demonstrate that for you!' He laughs.

After pursuing his studies overseas, Rajah inherited the tea plantation and returned to Makaibari with the idea of reinventing tea farming based on the superficially bizarre principles of biodynamics. Many thought he was completely mad.

The concept of biodynamics, 'healing the earth', was first put forward by German conservationist Rudolf Steiner in 1924. In a Europe ravaged by war, Steiner was commissioned to come up with a way of rejuvenating the battle-scarred landscape.

What he was striving for was the basic ideal of humans, animals and plants living together in a perfectly balanced ecosystem.

In Steiner's system, soil is regarded as a living organism – it needs to be kept healthy and balanced. The plants grown in this soil will, therefore, be especially enriching for those that consume them. This approach is not out of place in India, where ayurveda (the holistic version of homeopathy) and yoga (the holistic bendy version of going to the gym) have both aspired to a balance between the spiritual and physical. To further emphasize the Hindu aspect of it all, I discover that the holistic farming methods here at Makaibari revolve around the holy cow.

Manure used to make the biodynamic compost that gives Makaibari tea its special quality is not just any old crap. Certain rituals, or 'preps', transform the cow's dung heap into a living organism. Each 'prep' is performed in Rajah's garden, and I'm allowed to take part in the proceedings.

The cows selected to donate their excrement are treated exceptionally well, and given a diet that their Jersey or Friesian cousins would not believe. Vegetables, fruit and occasionally even molasses appear on their menu in addition to the staple hay. The cows respond by exuding a kind of gentle rapture as they live out this bovine dream.

The cow dung is then transferred to a large drum that is filled with fresh water. It is then stirred with specific revolutions, clockwise and anti-clockwise, creating a vortex through which cosmic energy may pass. Only then is it transferred to the plants.

I also spot what looks suspiciously like cow dung being stuffed into cow horns by a couple of chaps sitting on the edge of one of Rajah's fields.

'What's happening here, Rajah?' I ask.

'These chaps are stuffing cow horns with cow dung,' he explains. Aha, I think to myself and give myself a pat on the back, if you'll excuse the pun.

Rajah continues, 'These are ancient practices and are to do with energizing the soil … cow dung has many uses in India, as fuel, as building material as well as in this case, a kind of fertilizer … the cow horn is perfect for harnessing the cosmic power.'

'But,' I counter, 'won't any horn do just as good a job?'

'Only the cow horn is hollow and is the right tool for the job,' says Rajah. 'So basically this entire process is bullshit … cosmic bullshit of course.'

This is what you want from your cosmic mountain farmer, knowledgeable, bit eccentric and with a healthy sense of self-deprecation.

As Rajah enthusiastically carries on pointing out various fauna and flora, I notice an abundance of green leaves surrounding us, which, it turns out, is hemp. Cosmic cannabis? Mystical marijuana? Or just really, really good shit … man! Well that may explain all these crazy ideas. However, the pristine condition of the plants reasserts Rajah's claim that no one there uses it at all, as the natural highs one gets from the surrounding environs cannot be beaten. I believe him, though when I look round a couple of members of the crew appear to be missing.

As morning gives way to afternoon, we walk through the fields and I can see first hand the effects of these remarkable techniques. All Darjeeling teas are still hand plucked, and lines of women are harvesting in time. Two leaves and a bud, from every adult shoot. No more, no less.

This may be a bizarre, unorthodox approach to farming, but it certainly produces astonishing results. Rajah tells me that some years back, severe storms all but wrecked a number of the tea estates in the vicinity, but it was Makaibari that astounded the critics and bounced back and flourished before the other estates had even finished mopping up. We finally made our way back to his plantation house, where the fruits of his labours were waiting for our approval.

In other tea growing areas and countries, tea is produced all year round – however in Darjeeling it hibernates in the winter. Different flavours come over time; growth starts in spring with the first flush, a light, clean and refreshing brew. A couple of months later comes the second flush – producing black teas – darker and stronger than the first flush. Then there's the autumn flush, which is highly prized.

Tasting tea, it transpires, is like tasting wine – an array of leaves, trays, kettles and cups, an almost scientific level of preparation, a specific and precise vocabulary and, of course, a spittoon. Rajah explains the specifics of each tea, and how adding milk and sugar is the surest way to mask the true experience of the tea. Like diluting the finest wine, you just don't do it. I keep my scrapbook on 'great builder's tea I have drunk in caffs' to myself. The last tea that I taste is called Silver Tips Imperial – and it is the finest, most expensive tea in the world. The texture is smooth, the aroma is fresh, the taste subtle, and I'm left buzzing gently from the experience. I refuse to spit it into an urn. Apart from the fact that it is the finest tea I have ever ingested, I can't help thinking of how my Punjabi parents would be appalled at the thought of me spitting out so much money.

Rajah proudly and rather endearingly shows me the certificate, declaring his Silver Tips the most expensive tea in the world.

'Rajah,' I tell him, 'I did believe you, you know? If you tell me it's the most expensive tea, I trust you.'

'Do you? That's good, we farmers have a way of inspiring trust I think.'

Ironically, considering biodynamics is meant to be truly spiritual and non-profitable, Rajah has used his revolutionary methods to help save Darjeeling tea's elitist reputation, and there are other aspects to his work. The villagers surrounding Makaibari are offered employment at the estate itself and the employees are provided with their own cows. The manure is used as fertilizer in their own gardens as well as on the tea plants, and any surplus (as well as milk) can be sold. The manure also serves another innovative purpose – it is collected in a unit, a 'balloon', in the villagers' gardens that converts its methane into a renewable source of cooking fuel called bio-gas.

This practice is not only good for the environment but lessens the women's work load – for it is the women who traditionally get up to chop, carry and stack firewood before their day's work even begins. Indeed out on the roads it is the women who can be seen toiling under the weight of rocks and cement in the midday sun, while the men stand around giving orders and discussing the finer points of road-building.

ABOVE: Now I've had the world's most expensive tea, I await the world's most expensive biscuit.

Further to Rajah's own commitment to social advancement, the cows and small-holdings given to the villagers are passed down through maternal succession, thereby providing a further emancipated platform for the local womenfolk.

Makaibari also has a wildlife sanctum and is home to 'Project Panther' (the estate is home to this endangered species). Seventy per cent of Makaibari's land is under forest cover, and in 1994 a new insect was found in Makaibari that exactly resembled a tea leaf – Rajah's got one sitting nestled in the branches of a bonsai tree in his office, and is currently trying to get it recognized as a new species.

Both Rajah Bannerjee and his tea estate have a rather profound impact on me. The aesthetic nature of the land, devoid of the vulgarity that heavy industry brings, makes me feel tranquil in a way I was not expecting. Bannerjee, the 'Mountain Man', is charming, charismatic and generous, and possesses that rare quality in deeply spiritual and committed individuals: a sly, twinkling sense of humour. And what's more … he gives me a genuine Gurkha hat.

The tea industry in Darjeeling is going through a difficult period. Many tea estates have been shut down due to financial or managerial problems. One of the main factors in the decline of Darjeeling's tea trade is 'copycat' teas passing themselves off as the famous 'Darjeeling' and flooding the market. But this is where Rajah fits into the picture; he's living proof that sometimes, just sometimes, money is not the only reason for doing things differently.

India now produces more tea than anywhere else in the world, and Darjeeling has the British love of teatime to thank for its world-wide fame.

Jimmy Choo Choo

OPPOSITE: Darjeeling's famed steam Himalayan Railway.

Another living British legacy is the Darjeeling Himalayan Railway. Commonly known as the Toy Train (although if you bump into a purist, please refer to it as 'Narrow Gauge', unless you want a knee in

ABOVE: Riding shotgun
on the Toy Train. The
water, coal, fire and steam
make it feel more like a
living organ than a vehicle.

the groin!), it's been puffing its way up these hills for more than a
century, and today I've been granted the rare honour of riding in the
locomotive with the driver.

Completed in 1881, The Toy Train was the very first hill passenger
railway and is still in use today, carrying schoolchildren and commuters
from Ghoom to Kurseong and on to Darjeeling.

The original passenger carriage was a small four-wheeled trolley
with canvas roof and two wooden benches for seats. The line made
ferrying people, plants and building materials to and from the new tea
plantations considerably easier – before 1881, the main method of
transportation was by pony or mule.

The Toy Train was recently made a World Heritage Sight, only the
second railway to be awarded this honour (the other being the
Semmering Railway in Austria). The construction is considered to be
unique – the steep gradient and sharp curves of the mountain face
being difficult obstacles to overcome when constructing a safe and
durable railway line.

It's said that the construction engineer thought of abandoning the
project at Tindharia – some thirty miles from Darjeeling. The extent of
the hill's erosion meant it was impossible to take the line forward. His
wife apparently suggested that if it was impossible to move forward,
why not go back? It was his wife's remark that led to the Toy Train's

114

famous Z-crossings, a remarkably inventive idea whereby the train pushes backwards to reach a certain height and then continues forward – creating a 'Z' shape in the line.

In order to maximize the passengers' enjoyment of the spectacular vistas, no tunnels were built or bored along the entire length of the journey. Mark Twain, after his trip on the train in 1895, said: 'The most enjoyable day I've spent on Earth is of mixed ecstasy of deadly fright and unimaginable joy.' I wonder if he would've rephrased 'deadly fright', had he experienced a cab ride through a modern Indian city?

This is another example of how an idea that was essentially British and constructed during the days of the Raj, has been embraced by post-colonial Indians. There is no widespread, wholescale hatred of Britain or of her time in India, despite a total awareness of some rather dark episodes concerning maltreatment of Indians and quelling of mutinies. This sweet little train chuff-chuffing its way up and down these hills is also a testimony to India's ability to embrace its past with-out bitterness. It was British, it's now Indian, so let's now get on with our lives everybody.

Today the train track runs alongside and intermittently criss-crosses the main road, and cars, trucks, buses and scooters come to a respectful halt as Tej the Tank Engine chugs regally but slightly asthmatically past. I happily play out a childhood fantasy of shovelling coal and tooting the whistle while riding on the running plate. The space in the engine is, as you would imagine, rather restricted, and as I am the junior member of the crew, I am consigned for the most part to balancing on one foot, on a narrow rail on the outside of the locomotive. I wrap one arm around the open window and hang on as tightly as I can. I picture myself as a Bollywood hero or Douglas Fairbanks Jr., doing all my own stunts, until cramp sets in and I feel soot in my ears, but still … the romance of steam, eh? The cold, fresh mountain air, the glowing coals and the steaming water. Blackened hands and faces, the low steady rumble of the wheels and the pumping, driving rhythm of the engine. The past, happily surviving in the present.

India's favourite Englishman

The next morning, I wake up painfully early as the sound of a thousand chanting children drifts across the mountains above Darjeeling town.

Wandering up towards the source of the racket, what I find is a warming example of the pluralist India that I've heard so much about – a temple where Buddhist and Hindu deities live side by side, and priests of both faiths share the morning rites.

I know from personal experience in the Punjab how closely tied Hindus and Sikhs have been in the past, and still are despite the appalling and indefensible anti-Sikh riots that took place in the aftermath of Prime Minister Indira Gandhi's assassination in 1984. Within my own high-caste Hindu family, there were numerous Sikh 'uncles' and 'aunties' that were accorded family status. It is certainly fairly common for followers of different faiths to participate in each other's festivals, but sharing the same temple and prayers is not something I'd ever come across.

The local children begin their day with Buddhist prayers in an open courtyard, like a dawn assembly. The line of children then makes its way to another part of the temple, festooned with a million multi-coloured Buddhist prayer flags and brightly painted Hindu demi-Gods.

Here the children greet the dawn by throwing flour into the air, before making a circuit of the main shrine where prayers are made to both the Hindu and Buddhist idols, ringing the bells and heading back to the classroom to start the day's lessons. It's a beautiful, inclusive way of bringing in the new day and the only observers are the multitude of monkeys that clamber about impatiently, waiting for people to leave so that they can begin their job of tidying up any pious offerings of fruit.

The inhabitants of this region are an incredibly diverse mix of peoples – north Indians, Tibetan and Nepali refugees live alongside the last remnants of British Imperialism. Endangered panthers are said to roam the remaining tea plantations, while tourists can visit the old Victorian colonial mansions. This unique cultural fusion is shown by

OPPOSITE: Two monks blow alpenhorns in front of the Ghoom Monastery, near Darjeeling. Cultural and religious diversity is one of the striking things about this region.

BELOW: Pious primate – Hindu Buddhist temple, Darjeeling. The monkey told me he was an atheist but thought the prayers were beautifully written.

the array of languages spoken in the area: English, Nepali, Hindi, Tibetan and Bengali.

In this region, where Nepal, China, Tibet and India meet, the reality of modern India as a diverse and secular society is visible at every turn. Darjeeling symbolizes a promising future, one in which cultural and religious diversity is seen as an advantage rather than as issue to be dealt with, a future in which different beliefs are not seen as a threat.

This part of the world has a magic all of its own – a part of India that takes its influences from neighbouring nations and re-creates them, absorbing them into the Indian Republic while allowing them to remain themselves. Sir Mark Tully was for many years the venerated BBC man in India, and was probably the best-known Brit in the country. I'd always admired him and was quite excited to join him for a cup of tea. On a verandah overlooking the town, I asked why it was, after retiring, that he'd decided to make India his home?

'Well for a start, it's impossible to define what an Indian looks like, if you go down south the people there are very dark skinned, Kashmiri's look almost European, you come up to the Himalayan states and they look oriental … so initially no one can agree an appearance of an Indian … you add to that the number of languages and beliefs and you find defining 'Indian' virtually impossible. Unlike Europe, no one here asks you to be more Indian, in order to assimilate. If you want to live here, you're just another shade of Indian.'

Mark is a charming gentleman; he gives time to everyone who approaches him, speaking unhesitatingly in Hindi, laughing and joking with young and old alike. He would not look out of place at any of my family functions as the avuncular elder, who is at once enjoying the jollities whilst simultaneously placid in his own headspace.

'Has living here changed your belief system at all?' I ask him.

'I'm probably more connected to my faith than I was before, but the one thing India has taught me, is a certain acceptance of fate … they say that how do you know there's a God in India? Well, it's so chaotic that God must be the thing that's running it!' He laughs.

So India absorbs and accepts a very British former BBC correspondent, without encroaching upon his intrinsic Britishness. This is exemplified by the edifying potpourri that is Darjeeling: culturally distinct, ethnically diverse, and yet in so many ways fundamentally Indian.

This is, after all, a country that thrives on difference – its variety is what has historically provided its vitality and, most recently, fuelled its economic resurgence. Ever since the Chinese occupation of Tibet began in 1949, this region has provided vital asylum for poor and persecuted Budhist refugees, with the Indian Himalayas becoming the adopted home of the Dalai Lama and the Tibetan government in exile.

In the mountains near Ghoom, a monastery emerges from the clouds like an apparition, a silent statement of protest against the Cultural Revolution. It's become a spiritual repository, a safe haven for the monks and their holy texts.

ABOVE: One of Darjeeling's street vendors. I had a packed lunch on this occasion.

Indeed Buddhism and Hinduism share many beliefs and deities. Siddartha Gauthama was a Hindu prince, or so the story goes. After witnessing the suffering of the world he renounced his earthly incarnation, achieved enlightenment and became revered as the first Buddha. Over the course of nearly two and a half thousand years, Buddhism had all but disappeared in India until the influx of the Tibetans – and now another of the world's greatest religions finds its true home in India.

India is not so much a single nation as a million symbiotic ones, separate but linked and interdependent. Nowhere is that clearer than here in Darjeeling where north Indians of every ethnicity merge like tributaries. Refugees have their own small outpost, from which they move into mainstream society.

It is a truly beautiful refuge from a tortured past that the Tibetans have created here, and their small community seems to have contributed greatly to the infectious sense of peace the pervades these hill tops.

But it's time to take my head out of the clouds … literally, and continue my trek into India's spiritual heartland, heading down to the plains, taking me to the holy city of Varanasi and then back up into the mountains again – to the beautiful, laid-back town of Rishikesh.

CHAPTER SIX

Holi Ganges

The mountains form a jagged crest above the clouds, like frozen waves about to break. We're gradually making our way southwest by air and after a blissful flight, where my eyes remain locked towards the disappearing snowy peaks, we disembark at Varanasi, a city which has a unique place in the Indian tapestry and which reunites me with the mighty Ganges.

Its old name was Kashi – the City of Light. To devout Hindus, this city is at the very centre of the Universe. According to the ancient Hindu scriptures Varanasi does not really, physically exist. But I'm here and what's more, I may have just swallowed a fly. The truly devout believe what we see on earth is a pale imitation of the true city which floats above and beyond the physical realm and acts as a portal to the divine. For Hindus, this city is a sort of spiritual departure lounge – a gateway that leads from our world into the unknowable.

I'd visited Varanasi once before, many years ago as a child. Some of the more zealously Hindu members of my family thought that their British-born cousin would somehow, on reaching the city, instantly exclaim, 'Oh my God, you're right, Hinduism is the greatest faith in the world, I will never eat a chicken nugget again!' My demanded epiphany never arrived and I think they felt I was a lost cause, as I went in search of comics.

OPPOSITE: Varanasi, on the banks of the sacred Ganges. Come all ye faithful.

We finally left for home that time, when I said to one of my aunts, 'If this is such a holy city, then where are the holy garbage collectors?' We never spoke of Varanasi again.

Perhaps as an adult wandering about this crowded town, I might feel differently.

Not surprisingly, to the pious inhabitants of this city, it is the only place in the world to be born, live and die. Just by being here, the city's residents feel they are the blessed chosen few; they talk of the town's holiness hanging over the water like a cloud, and whatever one's faith there's no denying the spiritually charged atmosphere of the place. Though I'm not sure whether this has something to do with the fact that every time I ask someone, 'What attracts you to Varanasi?' they tell me 'The atmosphere is really spiritual, innit?'. I wonder whether I'm being taken in by the on-going hype of this being a holy city.

Unlike other major pilgrimage cities such as Jerusalem, Mecca or Rome, there's no distinct focal destination in Varanasi, other that is, than the Ganges itself. To be sure, there are plenty of temples and the city is also a destination for people of the Jain faith and Buddhists too, as the original Buddha is reputed to have given his first sermon on the principles of Buddhism here. It is a little surprising to find in this holiest of Hindu cities that there is a large Muslim population as well, and this has at times been a precursor to communal tension.

I find a small café and order myself a fresh lime and soda. This being a pilgrims' rest, there's no alcohol or meat on the menu. I leaf through the local paper, which carries the usual stories about civil issues: STRIKE PLANNED BY POWER WORKERS and STABBING AT RAILWAY STATION, 4 SUSPECTS HELD. My eyes widen slightly when I hit the entertainment page. Here are the usual advertisements for the latest Bollywood movies, but inserted sporadically within these are loads of ads for soft-porn films: 'The Gypsy and the General (A) – Adults only', 'The Vixen's Revenge (A) – Adults only'. These are, from the odd picture accompanying the ad, obviously imported movies, but they are showing in cinema houses. I look

around but it's not a subject I feel I can bring up with any of the holy men sitting at the next table sipping their mineral waters. I leave the paper on the next chair, where I found it, and take out my research notes to learn a little more about this strange city.

Varanasi is thought to be one of the oldest continually inhabited cities in the world, dating back at least 3000 years and some claim a couple of thousand years older still, but as North India particularly was prone to invasion and occupancy, unfortunately there's no structure that can attest to that. What is well documented is that for the last few thousand years Varanasi or Benares as it has also been known, has always been considered a place of pilgrimage and learning.

The city is built along the shores of the Ganges, and medieval palaces jar for position with countless waterside temples. Life, as always along the banks of this river, is dominated by the holy water, and pilgrims come from across India and the world to worship it. In Varanasi, the Ganges is itself a deity, and for the faithful this water can expiate your sins, cure all ills, and provide a gateway to the next world. The water is, itself, divine. To understand this, we have to look back into India's distant past.

The Ganges is mentioned in the Rig Veda, the earliest of the Hindu scriptures. The story of its descent to earth appears in slightly different forms in different texts, but there is a universal outline to the legend. It goes something like this …

Long, long ago the great King Sagara lost his favourite horse. Handily enough, he had 60,000 warrior sons, and so he sent them to scour the earth for his trusty steed. In their enthusiasm they dug up the whole earth and brought havoc upon those who crossed their path. Finally, they found the horse grazing near a Vedic sage called Kapila. Jumping to conclusions, Sagara's sons attacked Kapila, accusing him of stealing the horse. In his anger, the powerful sage Kapila roared and in the process burnt all 60,000 sons to ash.

An ancient legend foretold that only Ganga, daughter of Himalaya, could purify their ashes, enabling their souls to gain eternal peace. But

ABOVE: One of Varanasi's many colourful pilgrims.

OPPOSITE: A woman offers a prayer at the riverbank.

Ganga was trapped in the heavens with no means of coming to earth. Generations passed, the warriors' souls remaining in limbo.

Then a descendant of Sagara pleased the great lord Shiva so greatly with his penance that he agreed to receive Ganga, in the form of a pure river. Ganga fell into Shiva's matted locks and finally came down to earth. The river then began its long course over northern India, purifying the princes' ashes and releasing the souls of Sagara's sons to heaven.

Thousands of years later, no river in the world has greater cultural significance than the Ganges. More than fifteen hundred miles long, the river originates in the Gangotri glacier in the Himalayas (believed to be where it fell from the sky into Shiva's hair) and flows in an arc across northern India from west to east, before meeting the sea at the Bay of Bengal.

A waiter approaches, pen poised on notepad hopefully; 'Anything else sir?' I put my finger on the text so I don't lose my place and look up. The place is filling up a bit, a couple of tourists have arrived and the holy men are looking studiously at the snacks menu.

'Cold coffee please, but no ice cream.' The waiter doesn't bother to write this down and goes to attend to the holy men. I continue with my reading.

Day in day out, a variety of offerings are made to Ma Ganga (Mother Ganges) and Hindus travel from all over the world to bathe in her waters. The experience is extremely important for a devout Hindu and many try to reach her banks at least once in their lifetime.

Hindus believe, like King Sagara's 60,000 sons, water from the Ganges is essential in reaching the World of the Ancestors, Pitriloka. Families bring their dead to the river, ensuring their loved ones' place in the heavens. In fact some Hindus keep a vial of water from the Ganges in their homes, to be drunk if a family member is on their deathbed.

Relatives visiting us in London would on numerous occasions bring a small amount of Ganges water, or 'Ganga Jal', as a gift, which was a nice change from the usual tank top with leg holes, sequinned

chinos and, one time, a reversible sweatshirt with medallion embroidered on the front, but no more useful. There was no bloody way I was drinking that stuff and almost inevitably, after the disgruntled relatives had left, the 'Ganga Jal' was poured on some houseplants.

It is unfortunate that this holy river's waters, considered powerful enough to cleanse a sinner of past offences and cure even the terminally ill, also carry some truly nasty diseases – dysentery, hepatitis and cholera. Pollution also endangers the unique species of wildlife found in these waters, including Gangetic dolphins and a type of freshwater shark.

Though many bring ashes to the river, often whole bodies, half decaying bodies and even burnt bodies are thrown in – contributing to the shocking level of contamination. An estimated 1 billion litres of waste per day finds its way into the Ganges, making it one of the most polluted rivers in the world. This fact is perhaps less shocking when you consider approximately 400 million people live along its banks.

In 1986 the Indian authorities launched the Ganga Action Plan, a well-intentioned effort to clean up the river. Although over $600 million had been spent by June 2000, environmentalists claim the money was used on inappropriate technology, e.g. sewage treatment plants which need constant power supplies that aren't available. As a result nothing much has been achieved, and the campaign to clean up the river is now being led not by politicians or environmentalists but by the priests who revere the water.

The temples of the old city attract the prosperous and the poor alike, those who have come for absolution and those who plead for alms, but Varanasi's holy status also confers upon it another source of pilgrims – those who have come here to die. Ashrams for the elderly are numerous here, for if a Hindu dies here, he or she is thought to escape the endless cycle of rebirth and attain Nirvana.

As dusk falls I head for the waterfront, now crammed with thousands of pilgrims and tourists alike; this is obviously the place to be. The evening *puja* or worship is about to get under way. A young priest, no more than thirty years old, lights fires in several pots and swings

them around as he chants his prayers. He's accompanied by many voices who obviously know the prayer by heart and shake their bells and finger symbols in time to the chant (you have to be truly devout to bring your own finger symbols to the party), and also by a thousand flash bulbs: the tourists have found their 'Kodak' moment. A galaxy of earthenware lamps are lit and placed in the river to make their way down the Ganga, twinkling away, the water current coincidentally shaping this glittering array into a giant arrow, almost literally pointing the way to salvation.

As night falls, the burning *ghats* provide their own warmth and illumination; these are the lights of funeral pyres in progress. The sight of burning bodies provokes mixed feelings. On the one hand it is a sobering reminder of mortality, a visceral symbol of fragile humanity. Yet here in Varanasi, there is another aspect to that symbol, a sense of liberation or release.

For the Hindu, death is merely a change of state, a reaffirmation of impermanence.

ABOVE: Some Hindus actually drink Ganges water, believing in its purification. Call me a wimp, but I stick to bottled water.

OVERLEAF: Morning *puja*. Dawn worshippers on the *ghats*.

127

Once again, India shakes the visitor into rethinking his preconceptions and constantly poses as many questions as it answers. And of course all this lies beneath the surface of a city that, for the most part, simply gets on with living.

The young priest, brings his *puja* to an expert end as the sun finally dips over the horizon. The people disperse and the priest collects his pots and retires, no doubt to ready himself for tomorrow night's farewell to the sun.

As I travelled along the river in a rowing boat the next morning, the gentle pace allowed me to take in the extraordinary sights and sounds of the banks and I noticed something quite profound. I saw newborn babies being brought by their parents and anointed by the consecrated water. A few feet away, children were running, jumping and splashing around and within a few yards of that a middle-aged lady was washing her clothes, as her husband brushed his teeth. An almost stereotypically looking holy man was repeatedly immersing himself whilst chanting a mantra and within his earshot, old men and women were being helped down the steps to bathe their wasting limbs. Finally on the other side of a wall, the funeral pyres were already being constructed, awaiting their grim rewards.

Within just a few hundred yards, the entire cycle of life was playing out before me. Birth, life and death, the joy of play and the sadness of decay were all happily co-existing for all the world to see, with no shame or regret. I realized that the sensory overload I was experiencing was entirely my issue. It was my cosseted western upbringing that made me shudder at seeing life and death as cosy neighbours. The on-going cycle of life was just doing what it was designed to do, to keep on turning.

It was a contemplative moment before I set off for my final destination on this spiritual trek. A far less congested holy town to the north west of Varanasi, which for thousands of years was revered as one of Hinduism's main sites of pilgrimage – but then in the 1960s, Rishikesh was discovered by the West and all that changed.

Instant karma

We fly to Dehradun by charter aircraft, and for the first time I can remember my baggage tag reads temptingly 'Your Limousine in the skies'. Not quite the image I had in mind, I think as I board the tiny light aeroplane. No buck leather seats, complimentary bar, TV set and requisite barmaids from *Hooters*. Cameraman Simon and soundman Andy are already sprawled in the back with the camera kit as the rest of us strap in. The seat belts look like they've been in place since the 1940s. We sputter into life, and take off in a fairly jerky manner.

Our two pilots wear Ray-Bans and do not speak at all. Not even to each other. We all follow suit, realizing that conversation is impossible over the sputtering engine five feet away. There's no in-flight service of course, and pretty soon we're all listening to our iPods. The

BELOW: Sadhus (holy men) meditate at the source of the River Ganges at Gaumukh in the Himalayas. The sacred river flows down through the town of Rishikesh.

Beatles at ten thousand feet are a familiar, comforting image of normality and I smile at how appropriate my choice of music is and allow myself to drift off into psychedelic reverie.

Weed-hungry hippys blazed a trail across Asia in the Sixties, and Rishikesh went from sleepy mountain retreat to chic rock-star getaway number one. It was here that the Beatles came to learn from their gurus and write parts of the *White* album, and it was here that a generation of children called Tarquin and Moonchild were conceived to a Pink Floyd soundtrack.

Today, Rishikesh is a curious blend of hippy throwbacks and ancient belief – a town where you can join a cast of thousands in the dawn yoga classes and have your fortune told over a café latte.

If India has a spiritual heartland, then this is it. In the region of Uttaranchal there are several holy towns, but Rishikesh has always been one of the most important pilgrimage sites as it overflows with ancient Hindu mythology. It's renowned as a place where saints stopped and meditated, where ancient battles were fought and heroes born – and the history books are littered with references to this pretty little town.

Needless to say, the sacred waters of the Ganga flow through it and it's believed to be where Lord Rama, one of Hinduism's most important deities, crossed the holy river and bathed after his first night in exile. Once again, the Ganges transcends the physical realm and becomes the backdrop to a magical, spiritual world.

The landscape around here is truly stunning, and Rishikesh has that almost indefinable characteristic which many sacred places across India share; there's something in the quality of the light and the air that makes everyday life sparkle. Pilgrims share delight in simply reaching their destination, and as a result the pace of life slows down and becomes somewhat more reflective than the usual Indian chaos of urban life.

Rishikesh is an entirely vegetarian town (our hotel didn't serve eggs, milk or, inexplicably, hot water either), made up of five different districts, but most of the action, once again, is beside the river. Here there are countless ashrams, refuges and hermitages, which offer a respite from the trappings of modern life.

As well as acting as an important pilgrimage centre, Rishikesh is home to many important centres of Hindu religious thought, and birthplace to two of the main schools of Hindu philosophy – Yoga and Advaita Vedanta. Today, a steady stream of students from all over the world visit the ashrams to study Hindu philosophy, yoga and ayurvedic medicine.

Yoga, long before its popularity in the western world as a discipline of fitness and relaxation, was a religious practice described in the *Bhagavad Gita*, Hinduism's major poetic scripture, as being millions of years old.

'It is a universal method of union with The Supreme' says a poster. Whatever that means. I've heard that at dawn there's a massive congregation preparing to bend and breathe correctly, and so I haul myself out of bed to investigate.

At an outdoor area the size of a football stadium, thousands of people are already up and about. There's an orange-robed guru performing advanced yogic techniques on stage, and along with five thousand others I attempt to join in. The number is normally twice that have turned up today, but the weather is a little inclement and, besides, it's being telecast live from 5 a.m. I wish someone had told me that last night.

I find a suitable vantage point and flop down on to some damp matting. Glancing around I realize how ill prepared I am. Folk have brought down extra matting, extra clothes and in some cases even an extra Thermos.

The guru on stage intones us to lie back and raise your straightened legs and hold for a count of fifteen. I make it to ten; my neighbour makes it to twelve. I take this as a sign to make conversation with him. Breathing hard he tells me,

'The aim of yogic practice is to gain physical and mental control over the personal self.'

'You mean focus on the cosmos and stick your legs in the air?' I ask.

'Exactly,' he replies emphatically. He then moves his arms about in what I assume to be a mystical manner. 'One must keep doing this until one's consciousness has intensified enough to become aware of one's real self, the purest self, the *atma* [soul], this is distinct from one's feelings, thoughts and actions.'

I'm a little confused. 'If I take away my feelings, thoughts and actions then what am I exactly?'

'The soul.'

'But then what is the soul?' I ask genuinely.

'Exactly,' he replies emphatically.

He pauses ... such a long pause, that I'm not sure whether the conversation has ended or not.

'That is life's goal, to find out what the soul is, what is the purest us, what is our essence ... all our thoughts and actions contain ego, the real self is what's left after all ego is removed.'

I think I get it. He continues,

'The goal of Yoga is Samadhi, Moksha and Nirvana – simply put, it is the focus of the mind achieving oneness, leading to a release from the cycle of life and death, in turn leading to ultimate serenity or what you might refer to as enlightenment.'

He feels recovered enough to turn to face the stage and, along with everyone else, raise his arms in the air for the full count of fifteen. The guru's session ends with laughter, as he instructs everyone to laugh. There's no joke or pratfall, there's just laughing, and after the self-consciousness has worn off, you find yourself doing just that. Laughing. For no reason at all. And I have to say, the fact that you're sharing that moment with five thousand others actually makes you feel pretty elated. There are worse ways to start your day.

Rishikesh calls itself the 'Yoga capital of the world' with justification – guests have the opportunity to learn to play the sitar or tabla on the roof of their hotel, as well as take part in all kinds of yoga classes, meditation and crystal healing; and as the popularity of Yoga and alternative medicines increases, so do the numbers of Hindus and non-Hindus to centres like Rishikesh. This is exemplified not just by the number of westerners in tie-dye shirts and sandals that are wandering about, but also by the tiny signs that seem to randomly adorn the town. You can 'learn massage' at the 'Hermit Massage Centre with Steam Bath' or perhaps drop in (or is it drop out?) at the even more enticing 'Yahuda Falafel Shiva Moon Café Chill Out Place'.

After a while I began to feel slightly out of place – like the only normally dressed guest at a fancy dress party. But as always, in India there's another story lurking beneath the surface, if you only care to look.

At dusk, as the light begins to fade over the Ganges, Rishikesh's own version of the evening Aarti begins. This is a ceremony that has remained unchanged since India first adopted Hinduism some five thousand years ago. It revolves around the ancient essential elements – fire, air, earth and water.

As I had witnessed in Calcutta and Varanasi, bathing, submerging idols and making offerings at the river's edge, are all acts of worship, and down at the Treveni Ghat at sundown the number of monks in saffron-coloured robes beggars belief. Yet this ritual is not just for the devout.

ABOVE: Young monk in Rishikesh.

It's a truly curious phenomenon, but it seems that since the trappings of Hinduism were adopted by the jet-set in the Sixties, a whole generation of Indian teenagers who grew up during the psychedelic revolution, more familiar with the Rolling Stones than they were with Ravi Shankar, have rediscovered the ancient traditions of their ancestors.

Once disillusioned teenagers, today they are India's middle-aged, middle class – and they regularly take time out from their highly paid jobs in the city to get spiritual up in Rishikesh. Standing beside me at the Aarti was a software developer named Vir who resigned from a highly paid job in the States to find himself in India. We chatted for a while down on the waterfront as the Ganges twinkled beside us.

'I knew something was missing, and I was having some personal problems. So I came here, just to get my head together. It was very different to what I was used to in America. But after a while, all the spiritual stuff around me started to seep into my brain.'

'Did you feel any pressure to join an ashram or get religious?'

'Not at all, no. It's like having a whole bunch of great restaurants around you, and being able to eat when you are hungry. There's no pressure, but it's there if you want it. Nobody says don't go to the disco or have a good time. It's not like joining a cult or anything.'

'Many people regard India as a spiritual place and Indians as spiritual, so why do you feel the need to find somewhere spiritual … like Rishikesh?' I ask Vir. He laughs good-naturedly.

'Listen, if I want to take some beautiful girl out for dinner, I want to take her to a nice restaurant, with candlelight and nice music because I want the atmosphere to bring out that glow of love within, so similarly if I want that spiritual glow I come to a place where the atmosphere will help that. I find it here, other people may find it elsewhere.'

I like Vir. He's open, honest, a good laugh and he's generous in his enthusiasm for people to find their personal enlightenment. There's no evangelical zeal in him at all.

Before leaving town, I join the other pilgrims in making an offering to the holy water with candles for my family. Perhaps I was getting carried away with it all, but it feels as if the Aarti is a perfect example of how India's future depends on its spiritual and cultural diversity. It's a fitting place to end this part of my journey, and reflect upon the story so far – and I can certainly see the appeal of getting away from it all in Rishikesh, if only for a while.

Never mind the Pollocks

We rise early the next day, as we have to prepare for Holi, the Indian harvest festival of colour. It's a day on which the otherwise peaceful streets erupt into mayhem and everyone gets covered in paint. Seriously! I've been invited to a family gathering a couple of hours from Rishikesh, in a little town called Ponta Sahib.

As we arrive, the locals are being drenched in what can only be called a torrential downpour. The town's Holi fair had been rained off, 'The Wall of Death', lit up with a thousand multicoloured light bulbs, sat dismal and deflated in the empty desolate fairground. Some rather pissed-off looking magicians were dismantling their stall and the remnants of a musical group stood sheltering under a lip of ragged canvas the size and shape of a spread-eagled domestic cat.

BELOW: Holi – Festival of Colour or Jackson Pollock Appreciation Society.

We headed into the town and bought our powder paints regardless. Pots of lurid colour were on display everywhere – rain or no rain, this was the day before Holi and there was a captive market for Holi paint.

Holi is difficult to describe, but bear with me. Imagine you and your friends are about ten and decide to have a water fight in the back garden and suddenly the grown-ups arrive. Instead of being furious however, they are encouraging. 'Go on. Use paint instead,' they say, while proffering a tub of Dulux to each of the assembled rioters.

BELOW AND OPPOSITE:
Holi celebrations across India. (below) The ladies on the left clatter the boys as they pass. More out of noisy playfulness than anger and injury. (opposite) Spring being welcomed in Central India. How much legitimate fun is this?

Then imagine that the grown-ups produce their own supply of paint and start pelting you kids with it, but it dawns on you that the family next door is attacking you too.

Now imagine that this potentially insane situation was not just confined to you and your neighbours but by a remarkable coincidence everybody else in the country had had the same idea at the same time. In every garden and street in the land, people were drenching each other in paint. And not just you kids – grandparents, neighbours, total strangers. No rules. That's Holi. And in India for one day that's normal.

Anyway, the day before Holi is when all the paint gets dished out. I think over time they moved away from emulsion to powdered dye, which the manufacturers claim washes straight out – but let's not get carried away here; this stuff leaves you marked, and people in offices probably compare wounds for days. 'Check this one out – my grandma got me with a metal bucket right in the face.' 'Yeah? Well, that's nothing – my nephew stuck a bicycle pump up my nose.'

The morning of Holi was fairly subdued – the rain had cleared the air and it was a little cold despite the mountain sunshine. Trucks full of excited teenagers cruised the streets looking for victims, but I made sure I showed no fear.

I'd been lucky enough to experience the crazed joy of Holi a couple of times when I was much younger and it had always descended into elated insanity. The elders and infants were gently anointed with soluble dye first before the ones that were left, ages 6 to about 64, engaged in guerrilla warfare. On the street, one had to be wary of boys on scooters, with water filled balloons. I even remember a train being splattered, the metal bars offering scant protection from the sniper-like accuracy of one particular skinny twelve-year-old. The newly multi-hued passengers wrestled with the annoyance of being hit, and on the other hand wondering whether they'd just witnessed the emergence of a new cricketing superhero. One particular year, we ran out of powdered dye, and resorted to mud and, much to the charitably momentary annoyance of my aunt, we tipped a bottle of ink over her head. I think we've all got used to the bluish tinge now.

Blessed with this experience I decided to take precautions. My pristine-white *kurta* pyjama looked somewhat vulnerable, and the hardened salesmen at the colour shop saw me coming a mile off. What had started as a harmless attempt at joining in the fun had turned into a serious mission: I bought enough paint to cover a small football stadium. In addition, I added some fearsome-looking weaponry to my arsenal: a couple of bicycle-pump squirters. I felt like Keanu Reeves all tooled up in *The Matrix*.

I was on my way to rendezvous with the pleasant family who'd so kindly invited me to be apart of their celebrations. As I approached the house, a drummer kicked off and before I knew it I was deluged. The experience was something like being the beneficiary of a surprise birthday party, except that instead of yelling 'Surprise!' and giving you presents, the guests each attempt to cover you with so many shades and tones that you look like a chameleon flung across a Jackson Pollock painting.

I can't deny it, but rather than stroke my chin and study the assembled locals, wondering about their motivation, I joined in. You can't help it. It's stupid. And it's fun. What else is there to say? Does it mean anything? Not really. That's a large part of its appeal. The fact that it is such a great leveller, that there are no divisions between grandparents and young kids, between bosses and employees and between men and women, makes Holi the single most equitable and joyous cultural experience one can ever have.

There are various theories about why Holi first came into being. Some talk about the festival being devoted to Krishna, Hinduism's most playful god. Others call it a spring festival; others still a harvest festival. All I can say for sure is that it's a riot.

As I danced around looking like Austin Powers' wardrobe it dawned on me that this was not the spiritual India described in the guidebooks and the tourist brochures. In place of the rather stiff clichés of exotic temples and bearded gurus, ordinary Indians clearly have a more palpable sense of spirituality – one laced with a sense of humour.

The only element that felt strange was the absence of my real family there. The thought that they were engaged in similar tomfoolery in another part of India reminded me that just when you think that you are bonded and close knit with your family, there's nothing like a mass water fight to bring you closer still. Go on. Try it.

I had a great time with my adopted family at Holi and I hear the party continued into the early hours, but I had to press on. The next day I had an appointment in the capital, New Delhi, to embark on the most personal and daunting part of my expedition.

PART THREE

THE LONGEST ROAD

CHAPTER SEVEN

Delhi Dally

I was fifteen years old when I first travelled on a plane all by myself. My anxious mother and several family members saw me off from Delhi airport as I travelled back to London. Being a parent myself now, I can fully appreciate the long traumatic wait she would have had, waiting for my father to call and let her know I had arrived in one piece and without having caused an international incident. However, at the time I was consumed by both the excitement of undertaking something so grown-up and the embarrassment of being fussed over. Didn't they understand? I was fifteen for God's sake and knew everything.

Sitting between two obese, perspiring businessmen in cattle class, on a packed flight with requisite screaming babies, wearing my acne'd adolescence like a badge of defiance, I coolly pressed the service call button and ordered another mango juice. I was James Bond.

Thus began twelve hours of hell for all the stewardesses on the flight. As my surging hormonal confidence rose, I joked and teased them, seducing them with my yodelling breaking voice and impressing them with my Elvis trivia. They pretended to ignore it, even acted like they were tiring of my advances but I knew better.

It all ended rather abruptly over northern Iraq as I sheepishly handed over my well-stocked sick bag. I repeated this feat over Turkey, Bulgaria, Germany, the North Sea and Tunbridge Wells. Even though I haven't

OPPOSITE: A rickshaw driver taking a break outside the Red Fort in Old Delhi.

145

been travel sick for nearly twenty years, I never know for sure that I'm not going to have to hand over a full bag of vomit to a pretty lady.

This flight to New Delhi wasn't particularly eventful. I couldn't sleep as per normal but the chatty, attractive stewardess must have thought I was terribly rude, as I nodded nervously and continuously returned to my book. After a while she rather pointedly gave extra peanuts to the guy next to me and I think deliberately tipped coffee into my saucer. But on a plus note the sick bag remained untarnished, waiting patiently for the next spotty young know-it-all.

New Delhi was always the first destination through all my childhood travel years. It's the Indian city I feel most familiar with and yet I always see a side to it that surprises me and makes me feel like I'm seeing it for the first time.

This leg of the journey was the one that I had the most apprehension about. I wanted to understand the legacy of Partition by retracing the moments that led to it. But this would entail retracing my father's steps who, as a refugee, came to India from what is now Pakistan, across the savagely torn lands of communal violence.

This journey would take me back through those very lands and across the border into Pakistan, to try and locate my father's ancestral village.

The last capital of the British Raj, the scene of the announcement of the birth of India as independent nation, seemed the obvious place to start. It was also the city that my father and his beleaguered relatives arrived in, back in 1947. Now, I was about to embark on a journey where I would have to reopen some of those resolutely closed doors on memories of that period, and possibly rattle some of those still raw nerves. I was going to ask some pretty direct questions and I wasn't sure whether I'd be able to handle hearing about those terrible times.

I thought my starting point should be where my grandmother used to live, and where my family, for years, would descend and nick all her floor space. And so I head for one of the central areas of New Delhi, called Paharganj. The area seems more crowded than I remembered it. But then I remember that I've thought that on every visit here.

The narrow interconnecting alleys are congested with human and animal traffic, and I allow myself to be swept along with the tide. A blaze of colour in my peripheral vision turns out to be a man's head-dress. Shoulders buckle under impossible loads; a steel trunk, a child, two tea chests …

Along a (thankfully) wider street and I spy barbers shaving their clients at the kerbside, conducting heated arguments with their neighbours. On display are menus of the most incredible hairstyles I've ever seen, resilient head-top relics of the 1970s, though each customer emerges from the Sweeny Todd experience pretty much with the same look. Short back and sides, trimmed moustache.

The major difference I note from my childhood visits is that where the narrow markets were once packed with a mix of stalls and open-fronted shops, selling food, clothes and household requirements, these have been replaced with air-conditioned, glass-fronted, smart 'outlets'. Western brands from jeans to MP3 players sit happily next door to 'Bunty Footwears' or a specialist sari shop. Just outside these shops, even in the narrowest alleys, defying the laws of physics, food trolleys and stalls have set up and still can't stem the masses out hunting for a bargain.

Mothers and daughters, dressed in jeans, sandals and T-shirts, emerge from trendy coffee shops, their jangling bangles beating out a tambourine rhythm, making their chatter sound like performance art. Young lads, sporting fashionably long hair, congregate around the snack stalls, using their nibbling to mask furtive glances at the passing girls.

This is a far cry from the Paharganj that I was brought to. It may be hard to believe, but I was quite a pretty child. I recall how once in these very streets, a bunch of ragamuffins chased me, throwing shoes and calling me a girl. On reflection, perhaps wearing a frock was a bad idea. I'm joking of course. My 'foreign' clothes and slightly longer hair (it was the glam-rock era in Britain) marked me out as different, and different was not welcome back then.

The congested streets offered no respite from prying eyes and brushing limbs. And as if that wasn't enough, the chaos out on the streets was

ABOVE: Delhi's crowded market streets are much as I remember them from my childhood visits.

combined with an almost unbearable level of scrutiny inside the house. I was the reluctant exotic relation – the exciting foreigner that gets peered at, prodded and spoken about as if you're not in the room. An endless parade of family would arrive, test my Hindi and laugh at my accent before foisting *laddoos*, *jalebis* and *barfi* upon me – traditional Indian sweets made variously of sugar, lentils, nuts, sugar, condensed milk, sugar, syrup, sweet batter and sugar. To refer to these delicacies as sweet would be an understatement commensurate with calling the solar system 'quite big'. To even utter these sweet names in anything over a whisper is to invite diabetes. Of course they are totally addictive.

Looking back, to the warm and constant trickle of extended family that would arrive at my grandmother's flat I must have appeared to be a sullen little oik – but the only thing I can say in my defence is that one can only have one's cheek squeezed so many times before beginning to resent it slightly. Perhaps, in a Kiplingesque way, it answers how I acquired my dimples.

I would escape to the open balcony and gaze at the melée below, and watch the smoke billowing from the smelting plant across the road, longing for the relative anonymity and simplicity of west London. I later found out that this crowded part of central Delhi was renowned for drug trafficking and criminal hideouts, so no wonder I wasn't allowed to play outside.

Today Paharganj is a haven for tourists of every nationality, a place where you can pause for a café latte whilst checking your emails before drawing a deep breath and re-engaging with the drumming hum of India.

But no café lattes or surfing the net for me; my mission is more personal. Sixty years ago, when India won its independence from the Raj and became a separate nation from Pakistan, it was in this area that the refugees from Pakistan first took shelter, and my father was amongst them.

The story of what happened in the build-up to Independence has filled many a book in its own right, but if you want to understand why India is the country that it is today, the most important thing you need to realize is that the modern nation is a very recent creation.

In the 1930s, when the British first announced their intention to grant their former colony independence, the Muslims and the Hindus who made up the vast majority of India's population started fighting bitterly over who would inherit the government. The British solution was a familiar one, having been implemented in Ireland just a few years earlier. Basically, India would be divided into two new countries: the Republic of India for the Hindu majority, and the new state of Pakistan exclusively for the Muslims. The process was called Partition, and it caused the largest movement of people in human history.

In 1947, as the British ceremonially abandoned India to its fate, countless Muslims were also leaving the country, making their way to their new homelands of West Pakistan and East Pakistan (now Bangladesh), carved out of areas where there was already a Muslim majority. Coming in the opposite direction were millions of Hindus, leaving their ancestral villages in what was now Muslim territory to start all over again in the new Republic of India.

Estimates vary, but most historians agree that at least ten million people were displaced by the creation of the new borders, and my family was caught up in the mayhem. As a 16-year-old boy, my father joined the endless column of Hindu refugees from Pakistan and finally arrived here in Delhi, in the district of Paharganj.

My first goal is to try and find what remains of the spot where my father first arrived in this country. The crew and myself drive down to Delhi's main railway station, which is as far as our large vehicles can go before Paharganj's lanes get totally unpassable. Just a few hundred yards away from the main tourist strip, Paharganj remains much as it was sixty years ago, a confusing squiggle of narrow lanes and alleys. I travel on by rickshaw but the driver has no idea of where my grandmother's flat was and within five minutes, I'm totally lost. The rickshaw wallah does his best and we turn out of the winding alleys and into a much wider and better-off road.

When I stop a passer-by for directions and explain my mission, it turns out that many of the long-term residents here can remember the turmoil caused by Independence as if it were yesterday. An elderly gentleman, buying vegetables from a stall, overhears me asking directions and joins in the conversation. He tells me that back then, the whole area was a Muslim cemetery – and when the country was, quite literally, torn in two it was here that the new, homeless Hindu arrivals were settled. Looking around, it's difficult to imagine that these smart apartments and the fragments of normal life – the stalls and families and bicycles – all sit on the foundations of such ghoulish grounds.

This also tallies with what I have heard from family members; my father and the thousands of other refugees were told to build their own shacks and dwellings, and had to clear the cemeteries themselves. That meant literally digging up the corpses and coffins, removing the headstones, and then with timber (generously provided by the municipal corporations), building their hovels.

The old-timer also tells me that somewhere in amongst the labyrinthine lanes and congestion are the last remains of the cemetery

that my father helped to clear, and offers to show me the way. Passers-by also crowd our rickshaw, suggesting short cuts, shouting and pointing insistently like a dozen conflicting satellite navigation systems operating at once. I ask one of the young 'helpers', who I assume to be about 12 years old, if he was aware that this was a huge cemetery once.

'Oh yes, all this was graveyards,' he tells me.

'Did that ever scare you?'

'No.'

'But what about when you were a kid?'

'Not really, no.'

'Are you scared of ghosts?'

'No.'

'Do you believe in ghosts?'

Pause.

'Why are you asking such stupid questions?'

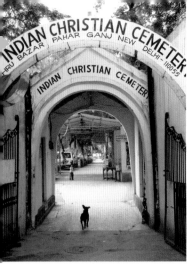

I manage to extract from him that he's not really afraid of monsters either. It's when I suggest a lot of people his age are afraid of such things that he finally reveals that he is 35, married and doesn't have time to talk to me anymore.

The lanes gradually get narrower and narrower, until we turn a corner into a wider lane and there before me is my destination. I have to say, it's not the most uplifting sight.

The remains of that cemetery in Paharganj now form a central courtyard, and lie just off a forgotten backstreet. Children play on the headstones and lines of washing hang out to dry. A bitch and her young litter have taken up residence inside one of the old tombs, and chickens happily peck away at the dusty ground. A gang of goats stare at me, chewing slowly like a bunch of extras from *The Wild Ones*. Old men interrupt their silent contemplations and sit and watch the goings-on inscrutably.

While the crew, surrounded now by the inevitable throng, busy themselves with camera angles and battery levels, I take a moment to wander round this area the size of about two tennis courts. Remaining legible headstones are replete with Urdu script (it looks like Arabic script), but the sweeps, curls and accents mean nothing to me, other than the simple fact that someone who was loved was once laid to rest here. The dates on the tombs relate to the 1930s and suggest innocence of what was to come.

Personally, I'm from the cremation school of thought. The body is merely a vehicle for who we really are, so what happens to our physical

remains is of little consequence but, nevertheless, the graves are a testament to people having been here and having made an impact on someone. Still, I wouldn't want to dig one up.

I feel a rising tide of sadness in the pit of my stomach. I feel for the loss, the loved ones who were left behind and then were unable to visit these last resting places, and the children and mothers who were presented with the macabre task of creating their homes in this, the most unfamiliar of locations.

Looking around at the multitude of observers, I realize that I'm the only person indulging in these feelings. These people have no time for such piffling sentimentality; there's living to be done.

Sixty years after the refugees arrived by the million, there are still people who live here in the cemetery – the flimsy makeshift shelters that line the edges are reminiscent of a shanty-town. But for the most part, the modern city of New Delhi has managed to push this painful part of its history into the most distant recesses of its memory. The way in which Paharganj has been absorbed and re-invented is a great example of the way that India is ploughing ahead into the twenty-first century; for in this country the spirit of pragmatism reigns supreme, and what was once the last resting place of thousands became a new home to thousands overnight.

Now our western sensibilities may be offended by the rather gruesome idea of clearing corpses to make way for housing, but for my father's generation this was not a matter of choice but absolute necessity – they had no other options.

So, even today, in the heart of the capital city, despite the cosmopolitan exterior, Delhi still bears the scars inflicted sixty years ago, even if they are, quite literally, buried just beneath the surface. But the people ascribe to a popular saying which one occasionally sees on bumper stickers: 'Chalta Hai'. So it goes.

A town within a city

I wanted to get under the skin of the city that my father was evacuated to, a city that was a seat of power for over a thousand years, a city I had visited numerous times but, I was realizing, I still hadn't experienced. I had been told that to really see the hidden beauty of this modern urban sprawl I needed to head into its ancient heart – Old Delhi. This is, after all, a country where ancient tombs are gradually transformed into roundabouts and the monuments of past civilizations are visible at every street corner, and in Delhi the outline of countless royal palaces can still be seen poking through the detritus of modern life.

This is more like it – at least, more like the India of the imagination: teeming markets and traditional dress, a million exotic smells and lurid colours. In many ways, Old Delhi is a surviving ancient Mughal town, hidden within the modern city.

What better place to start I thought, than the focal point for the many Muslim residents of the old town – the mosque?

Every Friday, this medieval town within a city bursts into life at Jama Masjid, India's largest mosque. This huge place of worship was built in 1656 and can accommodate over 25,000 worshippers at one time. It is a sign of the times that as I enter by gate number 3, the sign also says in a much smaller font 'courtesy by Hovel Autogas'. The imagination boggles. The sheer size of the prayer hall is exemplified by the enormous arch at its entrance, which dwarfs the Mullah reciting the daily prayer, despite standing on a wooden platform. I take in the sheer sense of history of the place, doffing my baseball cap in acknowledgement of the Emperor Shah Jahan, responsible for

OPPOSITE: Muslim men praying inside a Sufi shrine in Old Delhi. The Mughal part of the city is home to this mystical Muslim sect.

commissioning this impressive building, as well as that other little lean-to in Agra called the Taj Mahal.

Twelve per cent of the Indian population are Muslims, and India is home to more Muslims than every country in the Arab world put together. While there are some amongst India's Hindu majority that might not like to admit it, the Mughal emperors and the Islamic culture that they brought with them have had an enormous influence on India's national character – its architecture, its literature and its food.

An area of the city called Nizam Ud Din, a Mughal enclave based at an ancient tomb, remains unchanged since the height of India's Islamic empire, and also remains home to one of the most beguiling of the many Muslim sects – a caste of devotional artists called the Sufis.

The Sufis are a mystical sect of devout Muslims who use music to attain a trance-like state. Traditionally, they played in mosques or religious gatherings, hence capturing and holding the attention of the congregation is the art of the Sufi musician – and this amazing musical form is called Qawwali.

As Qawwali reached a wider audience, it moved beyond the confines of religious arenas and into more mainstream pop culture. Perhaps the best-known Qawwali practitioner was the late, great Nusrat Fateh Ali Khan, who during his lifetime filled the Barbican, the Louvre, and countless other great temples to western culture with his soaring voice and mesmerizing rhythms.

Qawwali is so potent a musical force that listeners have been known to fall into a kind of devotional ecstasy. These are the whirling dervishes that you hear about in the Middle East and who occasionally pop into action movies during an exotic chase sequence; their endless spinning in time to the music eventually makes their everyday world give way to a trance-like state of euphoria.

The current leader of the troupe based at the Nizam Ud Din tomb, also named Khan, leads the music with his astonishing voice, and for seven generations his family have been this historic shrine's musicians and spiritual trip guides.

Around the corner from the noisy, crowded shrine I caught up with Sharif (at seventeen, the youngest member of the troupe) as he and his friends relaxed over a game of carom, a sort of table-top billiards, but with discs instead of balls and your fingers instead of a cue. The café was far from salubrious, but even though I'd heard that this was not a safe place for non-Muslims to be after dark, there wasn't the slightest hint of any tension when the crew and I walked in.

I joined in the carom game and lulled Sharif and his friends into a false sense of security by playing appallingly and letting them win. As they silently sniggered at my wayward shots I asked Sharif whether the streets around the tomb were safe, or if they were a target for right-wing Hindu zealots.

'Communal violence in this area is not unknown, there is trouble from time to time, but nowhere is safe these days; but yes, those who

ABOVE: India's most famous palace, the Taj Mahal, constructed by 17th-century emperor Shah Jahan. Judging by the scale of this and his other commission, the Jama Masjid mosque (overleaf), this was a man who believed size mattered.

OVERLEAF: Friday prayers at India's largest mosque, Jama Masjid.

157

are anti-Muslim know we are here and they will drop leaflets and sometimes march nearby.'

'Why do you think they feel that way about you?'

'Well, Muslims in India generally do face some discrimination I think … maybe because of things that happened sixty years ago, or even before … some of it is because of what people see on television to do with terrorism in the world, but we are peaceful, always have been and always will be.'

'How do you feel about the future?'

'I am hopeful. Muslims and Hindus lived peacefully for many years and mostly still do; yes, I am a Muslim, but I am also an Indian, I'm very proud of both. There's nothing that says you have to be one or the other.'

I understand his point of view. I was born in London and was raised ostensibly as Hindu. There was never any point at which I felt those statuses were mutually exclusive. Conservative politician Norman Tebbit's laughable 1990 'cricket test' – which national cricket team you support as an indication of one's patriotism (yes, seriously!) – never even registered on my personal scale of nationalistic consterna- tion. I never had a problem supporting India in cricket and England in football and upholding the laws of the United Kingdom. Tebbit's test conveniently sidelined those other groups fundamental to making up

the UK, namely the Welsh, Scots and Northern Irish, as well as failed to understand the emotional journey of the migrant. Needless to say he also failed to address those good people who have absolutely no interest in cricket. I have always been, and remain, proud of both my British and Indian heritages. Similarly, young Sharif and his mates are proud of their Muslim heritage and proud to be Indian too.

To exemplify these discussions with these pleasant and unassuming boys, a few hours after we left, a Muslim man was stabbed in the vicinity of the tomb. I watched the morning news on television with horror. No motive was given though it was suspected to be sectarian. However, no reprisals followed and there was no backlash in Delhi's cosmopolitan streets.

Grand designs

Countless religions, dialects and personal histories collide on the streets of Delhi, and in the run-up to Independence some sixty years ago, this was the infernal chaos that the British were struggling to hold on to – a country so complex to manage that even the governments since 1947 have only just kept India from cracking at the seams and imploding in social, economic and religious strife.

Delhi's colourful past can be viewed most clearly through its architecture. Evidence of the Mughal era can be seen via the Jama Masjid, the Qutab Minar – the world's tallest brick minaret – and the mighty presiding Red Fort. The one style that seems almost at odds with the potpourri of buildings is that bequeathed by the British Raj.

Edwin Lutyens, a British architect whose fame had grown through being featured in *Country Life* magazine, was commissioned with designing the new capital of colonial India in 1911. His brief was to create a NEW Delhi that would be the very antithesis of OLD Delhi: the crowded alleys and frenetic bazaars had no place in the new British master plan. Wide, tree-lined avenues and villas surrounded by landscaped gardens became the order of the day.

With Lutyens' designs, an authoritarian and almost neo-fascist kind of architecture claimed the city, and driving through the heart of the capital today is rather like driving through Washington DC (apart from the cows, rickshaws, ear-cleaners and so on). He attempted to incorporate some of the Mughal features and local red sandstone into huge monolithic structures such as the former Viceroy's residence, which covers an area of over 300 acres.

But even by the time that New Delhi was inaugurated as the capital of India in 1931, the British already knew their days were numbered. Whispers of discontent had become louder; Mahatma Gandhi was causing trouble for the British administration from coast to coast and, not for the first time, these wide windswept boulevards looked out over a country in turmoil.

Lutyens' grand design for Delhi, impressive and sober as it may have been, would become the mausoleum of a crumbling empire. Today these Imperial relics have been absorbed by the new Indian Republic: the home of the last British viceroys is home to the Government of India, and the ancient gardens of the Mughal emperors are where the new, democratic rulers of the country like to hang out.

They're presiding over a period of unprecedented economic vitality, one in which India is poised to become a major global player. But for

every dotcom millionaire there are a million homeless people, and for every Louis Vuitton handbag there are a thousand outstretched palms.

Progress may be unstoppable, but it also has a price. You can see this most clearly down on the waterfront, where the developed and the developing worlds collide. Since the fourteenth century, people have been living here on the banks of the River Yamuna in makeshift homes. It's hardly an easy life, but it's a home. Now they are being evicted to make way for modern office blocks.

Yet beneath the city's seductive veneer of modernity, the gleaming IT centres and smart new metro rail system, the realities of India's labour-intensive bounty become clearer. Early each morning, in the shadows of the foetal shards of construction, labourers gather to compete for their daily wage. It's a bit like a human version of e-bay, a labour auction that determines whether these men starve – or not. It's reminiscent of *On the Waterfront* but there's no Brandoesque hero here. It's supply and demand on the most brutal, basic level.

Despite the frenzy of new construction, the true character of Delhi hasn't disappeared entirely. You can still catch glimpses of it across the city. Characterless glass and steel facades are often just a stone's throw away from a colonial behemoth or Mughal turret, the remnants of a fort or tomb. Ancient mosques and Hindu and Sikh temples dot the cityscape like pieces on a chess board in a half finished game.

As we drive out of the city into the suburbs, there's very little evidence of India's history – no colonial buildings, broad avenues or imperial street names. The Brits owned the place but perhaps they never ventured out here.

But the decisions that brought about the end of over 270 years of British rule weren't made in Delhi, or Calcutta or Madras or Bombay. That happened in a small hill station in the lower reaches of the Himalayas called Simla. It also happened to be where my father got his first job in the newly born nation.

So we set off on the road to the north, joining one of the great highways of the world, the Grand Trunk Road.

CHAPTER EIGHT

The Road to Somewhere Simla

The Grand Trunk Road, or the GT Road, stretches 1600 miles – all the way from Calcutta to Lahore and beyond – and has been the north's most vital artery ever since it was built in the sixteenth century by the Mughal emperor Sher Shah Suri who then ruled much of northern India.

Its original purpose was to connect the remote areas of Suri's empire, making it easier to govern, as well as uniting his capital Agra with his hometown of Sasaram, in the eastern state of Bihar. At this time, the road was known as the Sadak-e-Azam: Road of the Emperor.

Sher Shar Suri died after only a short reign but the road lived on as part of his legacy. The British then extended his mighty road eastwards to Calcutta and westwards to Peshawar, a frontier town on the edge of the Khyber Pass bordering Afghanistan, and they renamed it the Grand Trunk Road.

Over the centuries, the Grand Trunk road has inspired a lot of literature, most famously, Rudyard Kipling's novel *Kim* (considered one of his finest works), which is mostly set along this incredible highway. Kipling himself described the road as 'such a river of life as exists nowhere else in the world'.

OPPOSITE: Simla. Alpine hill station in a tropical country.

Today, the Grand Trunk Road is just as hectic as it has always been – this, the busiest road in the country, is the commercial equivalent of the holy Ganges. Here the 'pilgrims' are the merchants of the world and they have come to pay homage not to God, but to the mighty rupee.

I had travelled this section many times on my childhood visits to Punjab. As my family were always travelling on a budget, this basically entailed a bus journey worthy of comparison with Dante's Inferno. The old buses spewed as much exhaust inside the bus as it did outside. Very egalitarian. All luggage was stored on the roof, and at every stop my father would alight and make sure no one was making off with our suitcases, containing not just our clothes, but more importantly, the alarm clocks, chocolate bars, vitamin pills, whisky and Marks and Sparks underwear that would pass as our emblems of love to our extended family. The seats seemed to be designed to inflict as much discomfort as possible on the person who dared to place their buttocks upon them. I should say buttock, as so many people would be crammed into the bus, that one considered oneself lucky if at least one cheek found a perch. There was no air conditioning, so all windows would be open, permitting the substantial dust kicking off the GTR to find its way into the orifices of all passengers aboard. Oh, how I loved those journeys!

After spending three days dipping a toe into my father's first foray into independent India, I'm glad to be heading out of the capital city and away from the urban bustle. I spend the morning with my cousins,

166

having a quick catch-up and showing them the latest photos of the London chapter of the family.

I join the GTR just north of the city limits and decide to hitch a lift with one of the truckers caught up in an endless relay of goods across India. His truck is his home – garish, loud and just one of half a million that ply this route. He's a fairly quiet sort, slightly less chatty than Clint Eastwood in those spaghetti westerns. He tells me that he's a freelance trucker, decorated the cab himself, transports mainly foodstuff, doesn't like being away from his family but has no choice as this is the only source of income, but in not quite so many words. I check out the cab. Various deities adorn the inside and there appears to be fragments of tinsel and glittery paper everywhere, like the remnants of a bygone Christmas party. There's no CD player or even a cup holder, no fancy bed with portable telly, no chunky chocolate bar or CB radio banter that I've come to expect from these transport nomads. I decide it may be best for me to settle in, plug in my iPod and take in the experience.

Having traversed Indian roads and being used to the unexpected aspect of having to swerve to avoid other vehicles, people, livestock or any combination of the above, I think it best to strap in. But there's no seatbelt. That's the point I realize that there's also no back to my seat. The driver's got one, so I ask him:

'Excuse me, there's no back to my seat?'

'No.'

'Why is there no back to my seat?'

''Cos I sit over here.'

ABOVE: Truckers are free to go wild with their truck decoration.

OPPOSITE: Customizing your truck is not limited to India. Truckers on the GTR in Pakistan also give vent to their artistic ambitions.

'But what about people who sit over here?' I ask, pointing to where I'm hovering.

'They don't have a back to the seat,' he replies.

There's a long pause, during which time no explanation is proffered. Now I'm afraid to break the silence. I keep expecting him to at least ask, 'Do you feel lucky punk?' Then I can legitimately say, 'No I bloody don't 'cos I have an incomplete seat!'

But the hiatus suits me. It's a long journey towards the mountains, and I allow the terrain and glorious setting sun slide past my window serenely as I happily consume the entire output of my late mate Joe Strummer through my headphones. Joe was one of the most interested people I've ever met, constantly accessing and absorbing different cultural experiences. He always asked more questions than he answered and I can't help thinking how much he would have enjoyed interrogating me about my utterly surreal trucking journey.

After a few hours, we pull in at the legendary Murthal services, where weary truckers can sample the best home-cooked food in the north. This is a long way from the Reading services on the M4. Yes – you can stop for petrol, take a pee, and grab a bite to eat just like you can at home. But here there are beggars, a dancing bear on a chain, and whole lives are lived out by the side of the road – like an American trailer park in the Midwest but without the trailers, although I do spot a couple of Americans looking slightly bewildered.

I take the opportunity to sample some *aloo paratha*, a potato-stuffed flat bread, favourite of the Punjabis and available in every curry house in Britain. It also happens to be a personal favourite of mine and makes my heart leap every time my mother, mother-in-law, wife or in fact random strangers offer it to me.

It's a pleasant enough stop, but saying goodbye to my taciturn trucker I rejoin the film crew's convoy and we try to pick up the pace. The Grand Trunk Road cuts across Northern India in a bustle of life, noise and fumes, and several hundred miles from here it'll be this road that will lead me to Pakistan and, I hope, my father's origins.

It strikes me with a mixture of astonishment and horror that I'm now following the same route that millions of refugees walked during the upheaval of Partition, Muslims heading north as I am now and Hindus pouring the other way. The lucky ones had transport, like my parents, hustled into neighbours' cars and driven to safety. Millions, however, had to make the journey on foot, some travelling distances of 500 miles.

Just imagine that for a moment. Just picture your parents, grand-parents, children and as many possessions you could fit into a two-wheeled cart, embarking on a journey, walking distances akin to London to Edinburgh or from New York to Toronto. All the while not knowing whether exhaustion, sectarian violence, disease or the heat (it was the height of summer) would take your life or the life of someone dear to you.

The GT Road would have seen more than its fair share of death and desolation in those dark days in 1947. But today on my journey, it has healed itself and returned to its purpose of transporting goods and people at moderate speeds and with as much tooting and horn-blaring as it can muster.

I'm heading north to Simla, the place where the decision to part India was made, but en route I'm going to stop and see some of my family who live on the way.

Back to the colony

Karnal, a large town, famous for its shoes and Basmati rice, lies in the state of Haryana, almost midway between Delhi and the foothills of the Himalayas.

This was the town where the demonic buses would deposit me as a child, choking and weeping, from the Grand Trunk dust. My mother's family settled here after Partition and with a small enclave that included my grandparents and three aunts and numerous cousins, this was the place that I considered 'home' in India.

My father's older brother is married to my mother's older sister (an

Indian cut-price musical anyone? 'Two Brides for Two Brothers'?), and they still live in the family house here.

This particular house holds many memories for me. It was here that I was fussed over, made the centre of attention and pressured to perform at vast family gatherings. ('Oranges and Lemons' and 'London Bridge is Falling Down' were my showstoppers.) As a seven-year-old, it was also here that my family and I were trapped during the 1971 war. I still remember vividly, the childlike excitement of the air-raid sirens being wound up like an old gramophone player, the blackouts and the squadrons of bombers flying overhead. My family huddled around the radio, anxiously awaiting news of whether we would need to evacuate or whether we should get the dinner on. A fast military jet could have reached us within an hour, so I guess it was either legging it or having a final packet of crisps. Radios? Blackouts? Air raids? I'm beginning to sound like a child of the Blitz! Thankfully, the action never got near us, and the whole experience remains a fabulously dramatic episode for a kid with an overactive imagination.

Karnal was also the place where my cousins famously emptied the bottle of ink over my aunt as Holi reached its frenetic finale, and where, armed with books and comics, I would feel a respite from the intense scrutiny of Delhi with my grandmother's cramped two-roomed apartment and surrounding crowded tenements. At least at the Karnal house I could find a quiet space and absorb myself in my books and comics. Two of my maternal aunts also lived in the small lane, so I had a number of venues in which to be fed, scolded or attended to. My grandparents' house, now where my uncle, aunt and cousins live, was a three-bedroomed, whitewashed house with flat-roofed terrace. The 'colony', as it was ironically called, was a quiet suburb of the mainly agricultural town, and the surrounding houses were built along similar lines, all with high walls and large metal gates. The gates kept out stray dogs and unwanted hawkers alike. In the evenings, most residents would congregate on their roofs, catching up on local gossip with very little apparent discretion as they called across to their neighbours.

ABOVE: My parents and me (looking the spitting image of my own son).

OPPOSITE: (top left) My dad's dad. He never lived to see Partition. Perhaps he was spared the trauma. (top right) My mum's mum, a few months after Partition, calm and collected in the New India. (bottom left) 'Papaji' and me. I'm aware that I've been slipped a pair of girl's shoes, but it's 1966 and England have won the World Cup. (bottom right) Me, my sister, Mum and her parents. The 1971 India–Pakistan war has just ended, and we're finally allowed to return in London.

As I pull in to the lane, I see the house in 'Ashoka' Colony is pretty much as I remember it, though the communal grassy area that we kids played cricket on, and where I scored one of the greatest goals in the history of football after dribbling past a whole team (well, I was the only one with boots), has been built over. The house still smells as I remember it, a reassuring mix of mild spices, flowers and furniture polish.

My family greet me as though I've just returned from a space mission and I hand over the sweets and biscuits I have brought as bribery for hearing the stories that I know must be painful for them to tell. My uncle and aunt, known throughout the family as 'Papaji' and 'Mama', have always been like second parents to me. They were given as much right to reward and admonish me as Mum and Dad, and like them, they have rewarded and encouraged far more than scolded.

I feel safe here, but slightly guilty about trying to extract sixty-year-old memories that they have done so well to protect all us kids from.

After the obligatory teas and coffees have been served and the names of the crew repeated several times ('Simon' and 'Andrew' prove not to be a challenge), I inhale slowly and begin.

I first reveal two hand-drawn maps given to me by my father. One offers directions to his and Papaji's ancestral village in Pakistan, where the family had a home for generations, a small hamlet called Badhoki Gosaiyan where they spent all their holidays. The other, details where their town house was in Gujranwala, a city famous for stainless steel and, bizarrely, wrestlers. My father has drawn these admittedly crude maps in biro and I notice for the first time, that he hasn't made any corrections. A map culled from memories over half a century ago and not a single mistake!

I verify the maps with his older brother, starting with the Gujranwala one, pointing out the landmarks: railway tracks, a monumental gate, a major junction and a short-cut alley past a Hindu temple, that led to the city house. Then still further up the Grand Trunk Road, a left turn towards the village, passing an ancient *gurdwara* (a Sikh temple) surrounded by a deep water tank and their ancestral

home at the highest part of the village. Papaji expresses his surprise at his younger brother's cartographic skills and we all laugh.

A pause. I have to broach the difficult area of those last days of innocence, before violence and confusion became daily bedfellows.

'More tea?' My cousin cracks the awkwardness with a P.G. Woodhouse-style mallet.

I start gently with my enquiries, asking at what point he left Gujranwala.

'About September I think,' said Papaji, stunning me with his response.

I was bereft of words. I had always assumed that the entire family had got out way before 14 August, the day that Pakistan came into existence.

'So you spent about a month in Pakistan?' I spluttered. 'How come, where did you go?'

'Well, we stayed in the house. We thought it might still be all right. Everyone else had gone from the other houses; I think there were maybe two or three other Hindu families left. We locked the doors and stayed inside out of sight. We could hear gunfire and mobs shouting, but we thought this couldn't last and maybe it would just die down. This was our home, we were reluctant to leave it.

'I remember the day we had to leave,' my uncle continued. 'I was still in my underwear in the morning, when I heard loud banging on the front door with a voice asking if anyone was still here. I peeped around a window and saw a Sikh soldier, which gave me the reassurance to open the door. He told us that we must leave now, no time to take anything with us, and we were taken to an army camp outside Lahore.'

'What was that like?' I asked.

'It was a grim place,' Papaji said, a frown forming. 'We were only given plain *chappatis* with a lime to eat; after a couple of weeks we left by convoy and headed for Delhi.'

'What about Dad?' I asked.

'He was sent on, in late July, before the final days. In fact your mother's family also had been evacuated earlier.'

Mama, respectfully quiet during our chat (and simply shy) also now chips in.

'My father [my maternal granddad] also left some weeks after Partition, trying to secure the property and making sure everyone else had got out. He lived in a different part of Gujranwala to Papaji's family. He had to grow a beard and join in with Muslim mobs setting fire to Hindu shops.'

'He wasn't recognized?' I asked, my jaw crashing to the ground with all these revelations.

'There were so many Muslims coming into the area from India and their blood lust was up, so no one noticed another angry bearded man amongst them.'

'How did he get across the border?'

Papaji takes up the story again. 'He managed to get lifts from strangers that took him close enough to the border and then walked across it at night; it wasn't all fenced like it is today.'

'What about the other families, your neighbours and friends in Gujranwala, do you know what happened to them?'

'There was one family that lived opposite us, a retired policeman and his two middle-aged sons. A mob of Muslim youths were checking all the houses and arrived at their door. They marched the three of them to the local school and made them sit facing the outside wall and brought out a gun. Meanwhile another Muslim mob arrived and said, "What are you doing with these Hindus?" "We're going to shoot them." "No," said the rival mob. "Don't waste bullets, use a knife. Anyway, this is our patch, we're killing them." Meanwhile the Hindu ex-policeman, seeing he was the nearest to the arguing mobs, realized he would be the first to get killed, so he shuffled across to the other end. The youngest realized he was now first in line and he too shuffled across to the other side of the other two. His brother was now first in line, so he too moved. By this the whole trio moved beyond the end of the wall. With God's grace they were spotted by an army patrol and were saved.'

Papaji laughed at this story and I join him, as much with relief as with the dark comedy of it all. But there's a coda to the story.

'About a year later I was walking through Delhi and I saw a man sitting silently on the ground, head bowed, hand outstretched. He looked pitiful, truly pitiful. I didn't have much so I just gave him a penny and when he looked up, he was the youngest of the brothers. I didn't have the heart to ask what happened to the others.'

I asked my uncle what he felt about the people at that time.

'There was terrible violence, terrible, and committed on both sides [Hindus and Muslims]. People were confused and in a craze. Not enough was done to dampen the emotions, it could have been more ordered, it was frustration, the authorities should have done more.' He added wistfully, 'There was never any hatred amongst the people, just anger at the situation.'

'You know I'm going back there to Gujranwala and maybe even Badhoki, would you like to see those places again?' I asked.

'No,' said Papaji, in a considered but firm voice. 'I believe in going forward, not back, my life has been wonderful, I see no sense in going back.'

I pack up my Dad's homemade maps, and given the intense emotions of our chat and ignoring the fact that it's not quite noon, I accept a small shot of whisky. 'One for the road,' my uncle tells me. The crew follow suit.

We draw the line here

The Bhaskars of Karnal wave me off on my next space mission. Well, I am going higher up into the atmosphere, even if it is just the middle Himalayas. The next stop will be Simla, where the border of mayhem was decided and where my teenage father started to move on with his life.

The road to Simla veers north, and our ascent into the Himalayan

LEFT: The Christ Church still dominates the Simla skyline.

foothills begins. By road this journey seems endless, but when you compare our journey to that made by the British government twice a year during Colonial Rule, it seems perhaps churlish to complain.

The capital of the British Raj, formerly in Calcutta and then in its final years in Delhi, relocated to Simla for the summer months, the heat being too unbearable to make decisions that affected hundreds of million of souls. So everything and everyone packed up and moved north. Unbelievable. The entire equipment of government, the thousands of officers and clerks who ran the Empire in the East and their countless files, their families and servants, would make the long journey to Simla in the late spring and return to Delhi in the winter as the plains became cooler and didn't fry the brain.

Packhorses, donkeys and an endless line of porters would walk as far as Kalka Junction and then, after its completion in 1903, board the narrow gauge train into the mountains.

Even today, dilapidated railway carriages from 1947 are still standing in situ, as if waiting for a summer season that will never come. These carriages would later carry the corpses of those killed during Partition across the border.

OVERLEAF: Spectacular Simla. The hills are alive with the sound of … Raaga?

However, we're travelling by road and our convoy joins the endless snake of traffic as we turn off the Grand Trunk Road and on to the narrower winding road. Every time we come to a stop, albeit fleeting, the inevitable hawkers descend upon us. They wave around the same pointless bits of crap they always have.

'Plastic windmill sir?'

'No.'

'Hand fan?'

'No.'

'Jeffrey Archer novel?'

'Bugger off.'

I'm guessing there must be some tat wholesaler who supplies these guys all over India. I have to admire the fact that they continue to try and make a living, peddling this junk. Perhaps they're all university undergraduates conducting some huge social experiment, with us as the subjects, like the mice in *The Hitchhiker's Guide to the Galaxy*.

After an eight-hour car journey, we finally pull in at the Cecil Hotel, one of Simla's grandest hotels and the venue for some of the 'working lunches' taken by the group of civil servants that decided the Line of Partition. My father remembered walking past the Cecil, when he first arrived in the hill station just a few years after Independence, and staring in through the windows at the vast and impressive atrium, too awestruck and poor to go in. Papaji, too, remembers staring in at the windows of the Cecil, when he and his family came to Simla a short while after my father.

As the crew unload the gear I get my first real sense of my father's youth. The Cecil is the first structure I've physically seen standing that is a witness to my dad's journey. Not only am I seeing it, I'm staying at it. I'm taken to my large comfortable room, just off the massive central atrium, and walk straight to the windows and throw them open. The heat and dust of the plains have been replaced by a glorious, open vista and clear mountain air. I stretch and inhale slowly. At last. Space. Fresh air.

ABOVE: Local hotel sign. Can I have an ensuite double and some trousers for the kids, then?

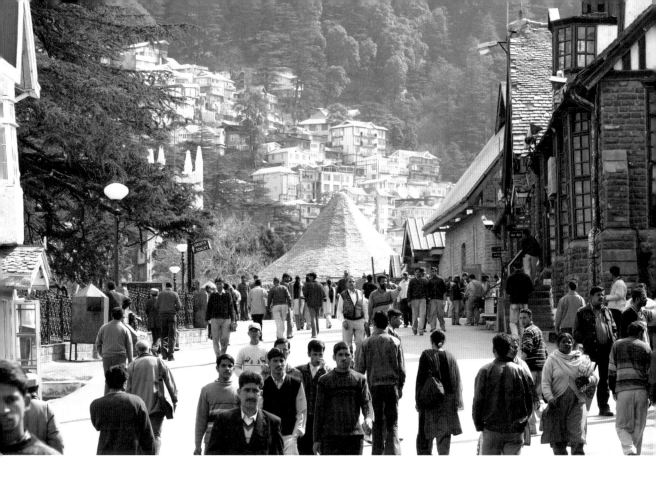

ABOVE: 'The Ridge'. Simla's colonial bandstand still stands as it did when my father walked this route to work.

Simla received very few visitors until it was 'discovered' by the British in 1819. It is said that the British officers were first struck by the 'cool temperature of the place', and Scottish civil servant Charles Kennedy built Simla's first British summer home in 1822.

Simla's reputation rapidly grew throughout the nineteenth century, and it became a very popular resort for British officers, their ladies and their young families. But a hundred years ago, not even the most prescient of visitors could have guessed that Simla's destiny was far greater than its role as a pleasant weekend retreat for the ruling classes.

The mania of the Trunk Road is half a world away from the rarefied atmosphere of Simla. Alpine Simla, with its mock Tudor architecture and its well-to-do residents wearing tight polo-neck jumpers and golf shoes. Simla, where the Brits went to try and get away from India, and where wealthy Indians still come to get away from India.

Closer to Rickmansworth than Rawalpindi, my first impressions of the town are of a pleasant Alpine time capsule. But from here, amongst all the kitsch and nostalgia for Empire, one fifth of the world's population was governed.

The town seems to cascade down the side of a hill, like a toy town flung down an escarpment by a petulant child, where the toy buildings happen to have fallen the right way up. Pristine churches, bandstands, temples, multicoloured sloping roofs – it's all here. Pine trees dot the landscape, people scuttle about wearing thick coats and woolly hats and just when you're thinking how unlikely a scene this is in India, a monkey screams obscenities at you and waddles off in a disgruntled fashion.

There's no denying it – Simla is pretty, so pretty that I'm slightly surprised that my father ever lived anywhere quite so picturesque. A far cry from Delhi and a distant scream from Hounslow in west London. In fact, I can't believe that he ever chose to leave anywhere quite so beautiful. I now understand better, those gruelling, remorseless trips to

BELOW: If Switzerland and India had a baby town together.

North Wales, the Lake District and Scotland. Whenever we had someone visiting from India, the Vauxhall Victor estate car would be packed
full of adults, kids, cases, savoury Indian snacks and fruit and the expedition would begin. I realize as I write this that he was of course
taking us to as close to Simla as he could get.

This town feels so calm and removed from the rest of India that
one gets the impression that Independence came and went here without any great upheaval. This is a resort town as disconnected from
world politics as Gstaad, Chamonix or Aspen.

I need to find out more about its place in shaping modern India
and I need to seek out my father's old haunts, as he pieced together the
shards of his life in a new India.

One man knows Simla better than anyone else: writer and historian Raaja Bhasin. This is his home, his kids go to school here and he's
the one man that may be able to help me clear up both matters.

ABOVE: Me and the
dapper local historian,
Raaja Bhasin.

Raaja is one of those debonair chaps that the British would have
taken credit for in a bygone age. His accent is surprisingly clipped, his
language and delivery that of a classical actor and he can carry off a
cravat! I silently wonder whether I should get him together with Rajah
Bannerjee, the mountain man from Darjeeling. Kings by name, dashing
by nature, duelling charmers brandishing G and T's.

As we walk through town, Raaja points out the buildings and
rooms in which the future of this nation was sealed. Even today, the
strict social hierarchy that characterized the British era can still be seen
in the architecture and planning of the town, with the church and the
Viceroy's lodge perched atop the ridge. The higher you lived up the
ridge, the more important you were.

'The rulers, that is to say, the British, lived at the top,' says Raaja
pointing at the skyline. 'The next level down were the administrators.'

'Indian admin staff?' I ask him.

'No, the British admin staff. You have to remember that the entire
government shifted here, that's a heck of a lot of people. No, no, the
Indians lived much lower down.'

ABOVE: My father's first photograph, arriving to work in Simla after being a refugee in Delhi.

My father had explained to me that he was sent to Simla to stay with relatives by the family. They'd decreed that chaotic, turbulent Delhi was no place for a young lad and so had sent him northwards. He had first worked here for free, distributing *The Times of India* newspapers to the hawkers, just so he had a reason to get up in the morning. After a short while, he found gainful employment as a clerk in the Chief Superintendent's office.

'That's still here,' said Raaja. 'Just round the corner in fact.' I feel a huge sense of anticipation – the image of my young dad, having junked the 4 a.m. starts and no income for the respectable 8 a.m. starts in a proper office with a stipend, fills me with retrospective joy.

We're in Simla off-peak season in late February and the atmosphere is placid. The Ridge and The Mall, where the Brits would promenade and take in the invigorating mountain air, is today half-full of local folk taking their daily constitutions. For the first and I suspect only time on my journey, the sight of a camera crew leaves feathers not even slightly ruffled. It's like being at an English seaside town in October or February and allows the myriad small shops to be seen in all their quaint glory. There are no street hawkers, no one shouting their wares. Even the newspaper seller, from whom I buy a sentimental *Times of India*, is too laid back to draw attention to himself. In the summer Simla is replete with tourists shuffling shoulder to shoulder, and even the famed refreshing air battles for ascendancy with the innumerable vehicles' exhaust fumes.

Twee, charming little Simla ended up playing a crucial role in India's struggle for independence. It was here that the beleaguered rulers met to decide India's fate and completely alter the course of her future.

Finally, a short walk down the hill finds us at the Chief Superintendent's Office. A grey stone building, accessible by a small bridge, apparently it hasn't changed much in the last half century. I instinctively head across the small walkway and into a musty corridor. Creaky floorboards and some metal filing cabinets, looking so old as to be venerated, all make it feel like I've stepped through a time warp. I see my Dad, striding purposefully across that same bridge, clocking in and shifting papers from the old filing cabinet and enthusiastically depositing them on the desk of an admiring superior.

On a whim, I turn down a corridor and peer into an office. This room at least seems to have been untouched by modernity. I don't see any computers or fax machines. Just piles and piles of A4 files, stacked haphazardly, rising up like tornados frozen in time.

Raaja beckons me out as we're not really supposed to be there, and in confined spaces a camera crew does tend to move around like a chain gang. We resume our walk along the ridge.

We find ourselves at the old Vice Regal Lodge, a grey baroque-style building surrounded by well-maintained gardens. It was here that Mahatma Gandhi, Mohammad Ali Jinnah, the leader of the Muslim League, and National Congress party leader Jawaharlal Nehru met to discuss partition with the last Viceroy, Lord Mountbatten.

Mountbatten, who took over as Viceroy and Governor General of India in March 1947, was to serve as the catalyst of Imperial withdrawal over the tense months that followed.

Gandhi was adamantly opposed to the idea of Partition, and urged Mountbatten to offer Jinnah leadership of a united India with separate Muslim constituencies, instead of the creation of a separate Muslim state. However, Nehru was equally adamantly opposed to that.

In June 1947, Britain's Parliament passed the Indian Independence Act, which set a deadline of midnight on 14/15 August 1947 for 'demarcation of the dominions of India' – giving Pakistan and India a paltry 72 days to settle their affairs.

The rooms in which the future of the nation – and my family – were decided are still here, still in use. The fateful space is now the Public Works Department, and it was here that the borders of Partition were drawn through the Punjab and through Bengal. It's an odd thought that in this room, which today wrestles with the maintenance of roads, bridges and sewers, the vast Indian subcontinent was effectively divided into two new nations – the Republic of India and Pakistan.

BELOW: Bridge of Sighs. My dad traversed this little walkway to work nearly 60 years ago.

And so in the late summer of 1947, a massive migration began, reputedly the largest in human history. Millions of people, my family amongst them, scrambled to cross the border in both directions – Muslims going west, Hindus and Sikhs heading east in the Punjab; Muslims going east and Hindus west in Bengal.

We amble back to the Cecil Hotel, where further discussions about the exact nature of the border were deliberated, over fine wines and vittles I'm sure.

En route, another little surprise. Halfway along The Mall, Raaja points out the Gaiety Theatre, a fine reproduction of a petite provincial English theatre opened in 1887. Plays by Shakespeare, Shaw and others graced its stage and, more importantly to me, it's where my dad went to see performances and himself appeared as a minor character in a couple. The theatre's front is unassuming and it merges with the shops either side. I would have missed it completely as its upper reaches are shrouded in scaffolding and, because no shows are playing at the moment, there are no colourful posters or bright lights outside to attract the eye. I decide to wander in and knock on the theatre manager's door. He seems only momentarily thrown by the sight of my face framed by a camera crew.

'Hello, I'm making a documentary and just noticed the theatre. My father performed here in the early 1950s. Would it be OK if I took a look at the stage?'

'Sure,' he says almost casually. 'Just be careful, it's dark, no lights.' He waves me on.

The theatre is midway through a major renovation and I can hear the work going on above me somewhere as I stand on the dark empty stage. The only light available is the few shafts coming through the partially exposed roof. I take a slow look around, allowing my eyes to adjust to the dim interior. I've performed on bigger stages and to far more people than this modest capacity, but standing here I find myself struck by a wave of humility. This was no arena for politics. It was where passionate actors spoke passionate words written by passionate writers to move, entertain and inform the artistic soul. And perhaps this was the root of my own future career. Maybe my Dad also looked out on these rows and small balconies, full of appreciative applause, not realizing that his progeny would be doing this for a living forty-five years later. Wow.

These days, Simla is a town that hardly engages with the present day at all. The picturesque hill station is the sort of place where not much happens, where crumbling mansions bask in lost greatness. New Simla, further along the next hill, is the usual modern blend of concrete, glass and economic over artistic construction. And thus eminently forgettable.

Simla has been a tonic to my senses. The mountain air has been rejuvenating and I've discovered some solid, physical reminders of my father's life journey, giving me a real thirst and urgency to discover more. Something tells me, this won't be the last time I'll be seeing this pretty little town, but the Grand Trunk Road beckons me ever onward, west towards the border with Pakistan. It was near Lahore in modern-day Pakistan that my family first started their long journey across to Delhi, and I'm preparing to approach the land they left behind.

CHAPTER NINE

The Land of Five Rivers

We pack our camera equipment and reluctantly leave the opulence of the Cecil Hotel and the crisp clean air of Simla. We're heading back down the mountain path road to rejoin the Grand Trunk Road, and on north-west towards the major Punjabi cities of Jalandhar, the border city of Amritsar and then finally to the Pakistan border.

The drive down the mountain is spectacular and hair-raising in turns; we turn off the engine and coast down the impossibly windy road with the windows down. The crew, Simon, Andy and producer Deep sit smiling in a happy stupor, lulled by the gentle hilly breeze, beaming sun and jagged vistas. Not many words are exchanged and I wonder if no one is saying anything as if scared of breaking the spell. We're descending towards the plains, full of people, traffic and unremitting noise. To underline each crew member savouring his personal paradise, all are connected to their iPods, lost in their own soundtracks. I join them, cuing up the 'Boss', Bruce Springsteen, to keep me company on our glide down the hill. Donning my shades and looking out of the car window, I get hasty glimpses of dilapidated villas on hills and pine-clad promontories.

It is easy to see why Simla must have seemed like heaven to those British officers of the Raj and their wives. It was, with its mock-Tudor

OPPOSITE: The Golden Temple, Amritsar. An oasis of calm in the chaos of India.

houses, its snowdrops and its village church, just like being at home in the summer.

A fair number of those same British officers, in the decades after Independence, came back to India. Unexpectedly, their posting in colonial India had taken them to a foreign land that they would come to love, and love enough to move back here when they retired.

My father told me of Mr Godfrey, who worked for Bennet, Colman & Co., publishers of *The Times of India*. He gave my dad the task of distributing the papers and even after returning to England post-Partition, could not get India out of his system. The last my dad remembers is Mr Godfrey returning to Simla in the mid 1960s. He was not alone in this respect.

The former rulers of British India effectively swapped sides, and became citizens of the Republic of India. Instead of being lynched by angry natives, they were welcomed with open arms. India, inscrutable as always, simply absorbed them. I'm reminded of what Mark Tully told me in Darjeeling, that the Indian culture is almost unique in its ability to assimilate change without feeling threatened. Astonishing, when you think about it.

Groom with a view

I wake up, disorientated and groggy, still in the back of a moving car. My shades are dangling down one side of my face, and wiping away a spot of dribble I look out of the window. We're finally in Punjab, the large north Indian state that was decimated by the line of partition in August 1947. Greater Punjab at one time covered an area stretching from Delhi all the way across to parts of Afghanistan and became a British-administered state in the nineteenth century. After Independence most of the area was absorbed into Pakistan, with a smaller section becoming part of India. Despite the partition and the fact that the region contains Muslims, Hindus, Sikhs and Christians, the common language even today is Punjabi.

It's a good ten degrees warmer down here on the plains, and the usual tumult of streetlife is everywhere. The sun must have fallen whilst I slept, and out on the mighty road, trucks thunder past with the inevitable sound of the horn.

The horn. Oh, the multipurpose, ubiquitous, impossibly loud horn of the Indian road. People should write poems to its greatness and its infinite variety. Some sound quizzical. Others furious. Some are funny. Some are sombre. In India, the horn is not an instrument of violence or abuse; every truck I have ever seen here has HORN PLEASE emblazoned across the back. To sound one's horn here is merely to express one's existence and to share that joy with everyone else in a several hundred-mile radius. Our driver expresses his joy every five seconds.

To the uninitiated or the incredibly tired traveller, the constant sound of horns is just one of the countless challenges of the Indian environment. Pot-holed roads, traffic madness, rogue cows and insane Punjabi jaywalkers don't help. And the street hawkers are back too: same crap, different day. This evening, amongst the usual vivid detritus on offer, is an extended range of paperback novels. I try to peruse the pile of books being carried while avoiding making eye contact with the purveyor. It turns into a scene from a Whitehall farce, as I turn away every time he throws a glance in my direction.

The book seller moves on silently and I resume staring at the increasingly glaring light bulbs and fluorescent tubes that border all the small stalls frantically trying to ply their trade to the endless succession of coughing, spluttering sloths that inch past their establishments.

People say that the convoy of refugees at Partition stretched all the way from Lahore to Delhi – a slowly moving queue of people 200 miles long. The traffic this evening feels a bit like that. I remind myself that at least there's no physical threat and I know where I'm going, so I benignly allow the symphony of the highway and the aria of the street sellers to wash over me.

While the word 'Punjab' may summon images of dusty plains and arid roads, this region is actually the agricultural breadbasket of India.

The word 'Punjab' means 'Five Rivers' and this region was famed for its fertile soil, creating a lush and productive belt which stretched from the foothills of the Himalayas to well beyond Lahore, before the fateful line of Partition was drawn.

My father's family owned large tracts of fruitful Punjabi land, which made them fairly wealthy, but by all accounts, there were no motorcars or foreign holidays for them. They were from the frugal, pious, work-is-life school of thought. Any money made from farming was, if you'll excuse another awful pun, ploughed back into the land. There was no unconditional trust in banking institutions at that time; money was simply invested in buying up more land. Why put your faith in paper money wealth when banks could so easily go bust, and land was going nowhere? How sadly ironic that it was the land that went. The wheatfields, undulating seas of sugar cane and corn, where generations of my father's family toiled and where my dad's adventurous childhood imagination was allowed to flow like uninhibited rapids, were lost to them forever.

More than any other Indian state, Punjab was most affected by the turmoil and carnage of Independence. Traditionally the homeland for Sikhs as well as Muslims and Hindus, it was the most densely populated area to be affected, encompassing several major industrial cities as well as the countless villages that were and remain India's backbone. Many of these cities had majority Hindu populations, but the surrounding areas were dominated by Muslims. This made the task of creating a clear and unobjectionable border extremely difficult. Hindus, Muslims and Sikhs had cohabited here for hundreds of years and, certainly according to my family, without the scourge of communal violence.

My uncle had told me: 'There were Muslim areas and Hindu areas within a town, where each lived but a few were mixed.'

I asked then, if people of the two faiths ever crossed paths at all? 'Yes, of course,' said my uncle. 'The markets and shops were common and also we had both Muslims and Hindus working on our land … when we left in 1947 we asked a Muslim family that we trusted to

OPPOSITE: Punjab.
The bread basket of India.

192

look after our house and gave them all the keys. We thought there might be a chance we'd be back, you see.'

Any chance at all disappeared with the arrival of the border. In Pakistani Punjab today, approximately 98 per cent of the population is Muslim, and in Indian Punjab roughly 96 per cent of the population are Sikh and Hindu.

The devastation of Punjab by Partition also had a curious side-effect ten to twenty years later – as a result of so many people being displaced and effectively not having any roots or ties to their new locality, many sought to rebuild their lives overseas. Punjab became the source of the vast majority of Indians who settled in the UK, USA and Canada. Post-war Britain, needing a workforce to rebuild itself through the 1950s and 1960s, opened up immigration from any Commonwealth country. Many people came to large British industrial cities like London, Birmingham and Manchester – and my parents made that journey too.

Arguably, those of us born as second-generation Indians in England are the children of Partition – it's odd to think that without that tumultuous moment of upheaval sixty years ago, my family might never have made the journey that brought my sister and me into being as the modern Britons we are today.

Anyway, what's clear is that around the world, from Southall to Toronto to New York, it was Punjabis who left India in search of a better life and a brighter future and who have put down roots and created some of the most successful immigrant communities in the world. Many second- and third-generation Punjabis are now electing to have closer ties with the lands of their forefathers, re-acquainting themselves with the further reaches of family and choosing to get married here too. What's more, they're doing it on a scale of a Bollywood blockbuster; no village hall or pub function room with curly sandwiches and fruit punch will suffice – it's got to be big, it's got to be bold and I've been invited to one.

Our convoy pulls over on the GT Road just outside the city of

Jalandhar, famous for its manufacture of sports goods. During the 1970s I received more cricket bats and hockey sticks as gifts, made in Jalandhar, than I had friends who wanted to play the damn games. In fact more than I had friends. There's nothing more tragic than playing cricket on your own and even then I never won. Anyway, I digress. We're only about an hour away from Amritsar and the Pakistan border and I can't resist stopping to see this fusion of the traditional and the modern. The bride and groom are second-generation Brits from Walsall, the home-town of my in-laws, and having had their civil ceremony back in Blighty, they're looking to party on at their reception here in Jalandhar.

Any Indian wedding is an ambitious production number, and this one is no exception. The venue is a purpose-built 'themed' function suite and it's situated right on the GT Road. The theme becomes clear as we approach the address – the whole place is done out like a fort,

ABOVE: Bhangra dancing is compulspory by law at any Punjabi function, weddings, festivals, etc. At least, that's what my cousins told me when I was a kid.

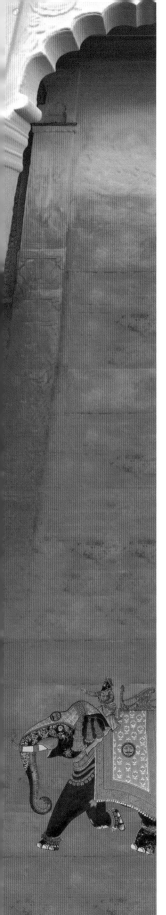

complete with five-storey-high towers and turrets. We've arrived early so we can find out what goes into the preparations for a wedding catering for 5,000 guests. Yes. Just in case you're the kind of reader that doesn't like to go backwards, let me tell you that number again – 5,000.

The place is still being set up; tables and chairs are being carried into place in the vast outside dining area and the various buffet areas are being readied. The most frenetic corner of this massive undertaking right now are the kitchens. I walk through a huge indoor dining area (nice to have the choice), which has an army of little workers polishing chandeliers, putting up streamers and pouring flower petals into table centre pieces. It looks like a wildlife documentary, particularly as there are, it seems, three people to every job. I can hear David Attenborough's voiceover:

'The worker ants scurry about their business with nary a word, their finely honed instincts carrying them to their destinations, three to a garland, four to a porcelain figurine; there are no written or verbal instructions save for the one that the manager ant gives by the rubbing of his antennae.'

As I wander through into the kitchens, everything goes momentarily black as my eyes adjust from the brightness of the cavernous dining room. The cooking area is huge and dark and it feels like I'm entering some medieval cave. Slivers of light filter through the windows on two sides of this irregular-shaped room and are immediately diffused by the smoke, from what seems like forty gas fires. One area seems to be for washing, chopping and peeling before being passed down a production line to the marinating and dunking section, before being scuttled off to the frying, boiling, baking, grilling part of the operation. Small channels are cut into the floor, criss-crossing the room like Venetian canals with tiny bits of peel bobbing along like gondolas.

There must be over a hundred people in here, but the speed at which pots, plates and trays are despatched and the general lack of illumination makes me unsure as to whether I've counted people twice, or simply missed the other hundred chefs toiling away. Was that two small people carrying that large tray or was it one large person carrying two smaller trays? The enclosed space and numerous blazes make the room much hotter than I expected, but the bouquet thrown up by this hapless combination of smells is rather delightful.

The noise too, seems reminiscent of a medieval scene, the clanking and clanging of stainless steel, like that of knights preparing for battle amid the various war cries:

'Chopping chopping chopping'

'More oil'

'Aloo gobi lau'

'Chicken ready?'

Cry snacks for Harry and for England, I think as I retire to the relative cool of the 90-degree heat outside.

The grassy area surrounded by the faux walls and towers is the main dining area for the guests. A stage is already erected from where the live music, and ultimately the disco, will be conducted. However, first the waiting staff must be hired. The first batch of hopefuls arrive for selection. They wear their own black shoes and this becomes the first criterion for elimination; the trainers, sneakers and sandal wearers are summarily dismissed and the chosen ones are guided to the barber, who sits outside the ersatz citadel, at a small table with no mirror, looking like a bored usher at a cinema kiosk. After being shaved and sheared, the recruits are handed their regulation white shirt, bow tie (elasticated, natch!) and apron and head for the final hurdle … the inspection. Like a military review, the boss walks up and down checking the state of these hapless (relatively) few. Some are sent forth to have their shoes polished, trouser hems stitched and one doesn't make it, as he couldn't work out how the elasticated bow tie worked, which seemed harsh, but how could this man be trusted with vats of hot *dhal* the size of military satellite dishes? It's tough and ruthless and he had to go.

Our camera crew decide to get a fancy shot from on top of the turreted towers until they're told that the entire edifice might come down if someone actually stood on it. The crew also then find themselves face to face with perhaps the most resolutely consistent feature of Indian weddings in the last quarter of a century: the wedding video camera man.

From the moment that the Lumière brothers brought their 'cinematographe' device to Bombay in 1896, I am convinced that someone in the crowd must have been thinking, Moving pictures eh? Stories … no, documentaries … no, news … no, weddings … YES!

Of course, Bollywood being such an integral part of Indian heritage meant that, as video cameras became available, a million unconnected Indians around the world became would be filmmakers, but never got further than weddings. In the pioneering days of the portable video camera back in the 1980s, a video-camera crew would push and barge guests to get the shot they wanted, shouting 'Hut, hut, video wallah!' in the same tone that cops in movies shouted 'OK, everyone back, I'm a police officer!' They would knock aside old people and children, forging forward like the Spanish Inquisition, fuelled by a greater moral and righteous purpose – the wedding video.

Back at the Jalandhar wedding, the video camera man and his crew (two assistants, one tall, one small) walked through the main gates of the fort and immediately set up their equipment, which consisted of sticking the camera on a tripod and attaching a big light to the top. As 'Director Sahib', as he was called by his minions, turned to survey his 'set', he suddenly caught sight of us. He realized that we weren't a rival wedding-video outfit as soon as he registered our high-definition camera. Director Sahib's pupils dilated in awe, and he and his assistants then rushed over to pose with our HD camera like it was a national monument.

However, the guests were beginning to arrive and I wanted to catch up with the bride and her family on the big day, before they were swamped by the 5,000 well wishers.

In guest quarters within the venue, the bride – Rajinder Kaur, a lawyer from the west midlands is going through her final checklist. Between checking her make up and laughing with her family, she tells me the reason for having the wedding here.

'I come to India every year and when we saw this place, I realized it was affordable enough to have my dream wedding. We couldn't do anything on this scale back home, it was easier to fly the family out and they could have a holiday too.'

A crescendo of drums outside seems to announce the imminent arrival of the groom, so I hurriedly leave the radiant bride and her entourage behind and join the others outside the fortress gates. Traditionally, the Indian groom arrives on a white mare, accompanied by a brass band, *dhol* drums and friends dancing as wildly as the law allows. However, as this is a modern hybrid wedding, things are done slightly differently. The groom arrives in a stretched limo heralded by kilted bagpipers. I can't quite place the tartan, what Scottish clan are they? McBhogal? McSandhu?

The groom, Tarvinder Singh, however, is resplendent in traditional *desi* wedding gear – long Sherwani coat and matrimonial turban.

I clock where I am for a moment. Indian bagpipers, stretch Cadillac, life-size make-believe fort, couple from England, all on the GT Road in Punjab. Fantastic.

199

This event has just started and though I would love to see the festivities out, we have to move on to Amritsar, closer to the Pakistan border. As we pack up and load our gear, a gentleman approaches and begs me to see the attraction next door to the fort and offers to give me a quick tour of the mini theme park. The theme, would you believe, is 'Indian village'. An area the size of a couple of tennis courts is given over to re-create 'an authentic' rural scene. Shoddy mannequins depict exciting pastimes including sewing, reading books and also cooking. The only live and moving exhibit is a bullock slowly walking round a wheat thresher.

'Wow!' I say with as much polite enthusiasm as I can muster. The bullock shoots me a glance, which says, 'Don't humour me. Just don't. OK?'

I'm out of the theme park before the vans are packed. The Disney Corporation must be quaking in their cartoon boots. As we drive away I catch sight of Director Sahib, halogen light blazing, marshalling the guests like Cecil B. DeMille.

Pool of the Immortal Nectar

It's early evening as we head back on to the trusty GT Road and onwards to Amritsar, holy town to India's 16 million Sikhs. I haven't got long as we have an early border crossing tomorrow morning, but I simply cannot miss the opportunity to see the Sikh holiest shrine, the Golden Temple.

As we drive into the city's outer limits, it's easy to tell that this is an affluent city. Amritsar was, until the 1960s, mainly a rural town but engineering and light industry began to develop rapidly. The suburbs are well ordered and the mainly Sikh population's egalitarian beliefs suggest that there are fewer beggars here.

We check into our hotel as dusk descends. The foyer is filled with a bevy of beautiful women. Now that's what I call a welcome! They are in fact the crew of a Singapore Airline's flight, stationed at the

hotel overnight. It's an example of Amritsar's increasing importance as a destination over the last decade and the fact that Punjab's overseas community have done well financially, that many international airlines now fly directly in to the city. One of the stewardesses smiles at me and recognizes me from my TV shows. Within sixty seconds, I'm surrounded by all the girls in a photo opportunity. Once again, I live out a James Bond fantasy. The fantasy (regrettably) is short lived and we head out to the Golden Temple.

'Amritsar' translates in Punjabi as 'Pool of the Immortal Nectar' and in the middle of a manmade water tank in the centre of the city lies the Golden Temple itself.

The Sikh religion was founded in the fifteenth century by Guru Nanak Dev who, like Buddha, was born a Hindu and after an epiphany began his own spiritual instruction. Once again, as with Buddhism, there are many similarities with Hinduism – strict practitioners are vegetarian, meditation is a fundamental practice, converts from other religions are not pursued, and spiritual fulfilment not leading to heaven or hell are just some of the beliefs that are shared. Guru Nanak's teachings rejected the caste system, talked of the emancipation of women and rejected the worshipping of lurid idols.

As other Guru's teachings also became incorporated into Sikhism, more warrior-like aspects emerged, including the carrying of swords and uncut hair being bound up in turbans. Sikhs developed a martial philosophy based on defence rather than expansion and fought fierce battles against the Mughals, and during the nineteenth century against the British. Though pilgrimage was never essential within the teachings, the Golden Temple at Amritsar has become as important a focus for Sikhs as Varanasi is for Hindus and Mecca is for Muslims.

The Golden Temple, an ornate and beautiful shrine made of marble and topped with gold leaf, rises from the holy lake and contains the Sikhs' holy book, called 'The Guru Granth Sahib'. The rest of the complex is made up of long marble buildings that emanate a cool, placid air. I join the devotees and tourists wandering through the vast

OVERLEAF: Amritsar. The Pool of the Immortal Nectar reflecting the Sikhs' holiest shrine.

central area, having washed our feet and covered our heads. The evening *Kirtan*, the singing of Sikh hymns, provides a melodious musical bed to wander about and introspect to. Such is the respectful nature of the religion that some of the hymns were even written by Hindus and Muslim Sufis.

Here in Amritsar, I'm as physically close as I've ever been to the Pakistani border and it was here that some of the worst violence ensued during the last days of the Empire. The city of Lahore (in Pakistan) is only sixty miles away, and Amritsar's proximity to the India/Pakistan border made it a particularly dangerous fighting ground during Partition in 1947. Muslims, who made up nearly half the population of the city, fought bitterly with Hindus and Sikhs. This civil war is reported to have lasted five months, but there is no way of counting the number of lives lost.

At the Golden Temple, I met a man, only slightly older than my father, who told me of his experiences of those turbulent times. Bal Bahadur Singh was a child in 1947, and hailed from a village in the north west of the Punjab. The modestly sized Sikh community there had been used to living in an overwhelmingly Muslim area, but there had never been any trouble.

As word of communal and civil unrest in neighbouring villages began to reach the inhabitants of BB Singh's district, tensions there also began to escalate. Muslim mobs began to approach and surround the village. Then began the attacks. The local Sikh priest was hacked up, bit by bit, as he continued to refuse to convert to Islam; a woman was physically ripped apart; and very quickly there was a deadly standoff.

BB Singh's father was the head man of the village.

'As the village elder, my father was respected and trusted by all; everybody would do whatever he asked them to, without question. Our village was surrounded by thousands of Muslims who either wanted us to convert or die … my father and the elders decided that they would fight to the death, and death was inevitable for us because of the numbers against us.

ABOVE: Young worshippers enjoying the ornate splendour of The Golden Temple.

'My father's biggest concern was for the women and children, and it was decided that protecting their honour was the most important thing ... as we knew that we could not survive, my father suggested that all the women and children should die rather than fall into the mob's hands ... My sister stepped forward first and asked my father to kill her first, so she could set the example. I remember she moved her plaits out of the way so his sword would have no obstacle in reaching her neck.'

I have never interviewed someone before where my hands have involuntarily covered my mouth and I don't even remember doing it, but both of my hands were now clasped tightly around my mouth. Stifling a silent scream perhaps? Maybe even stopping myself from

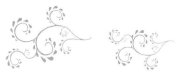

being sick, I'm still not sure, but I felt that BB Singh needed to have this tale heard, and I needed to hear it. I was way, way out of my comfort zone and struggled to ask him what happened next.

'My father then killed my other sisters and my mother. Most women and children jumped into the well; maybe hundreds died that way.'

I search for any sign of trauma behind BB Singh's eyes but I can't tell. I see the water sparkling and reflected in the golden glow of the temple's dome. 'Did any women survive?' I ask.

'Two survived. There were two younger girls that leaped into the well; there were so many bodies in there that they landed on top of them.'

'Looking back and the fact that at least two women survived, do you think the situation could have been handled better?'

'No, it was only when the Muslim mob saw us killing our women, that they turned away; then they knew they couldn't convert us, they thought, "If they can do that, then there is nothing we can do," and they went away … then those of us who survived made our way to India.'

The horrific images were filling every iota of space in my mind as I focused on asking the next question.

'What do you feel towards those people, the people that put you in that terrible situation?'

'It was a terrible, terrible thing, but it's important to not let hate fill your heart. I had awful nightmares for years, but the Partition was not brought about by any of us, but everyone responded to it in their own way … in life you have to deal with what is in front of you and what is real. We'd had many dealings with Muslims before 1947 and so it cannot be right to hate all Muslims because of what a few were doing, and also hating now doesn't change the past.'

I tell BB Singh that I'm crossing the border tomorrow and will try and find my father's ancestral village of Badhoki Gosaiyan, I ask him if he could ever make the journey back to his old village. To my utter surprise, he tells me that he's already done it.

'I went back a few years ago, back to that same village, I just

wanted to see the place, pay my respects, that's all. Of course I was apprehensive about going, but when I got there, the entire village and people from the surrounding district had come out to greet me. They all wanted me to eat at their house or visit them. Some even remembered me and my family and talked about how respected my father was in the surrounding areas. I was very moved; they gave me presents to take back to India. I got very emotional.'

I finally ask Mr Singh if he would ever go back.

'Maybe,' he answers, thoughtfully. 'But I don't feel that need to go now. I've made my peace and others should do the same. If I can do it, given what I have been through, then others should too.'

BB Singh heads off home and I feel I need to take a moment after all these revelations. I wander around the Golden Temple complex. Mr Singh's elegance, generosity and profound forgiveness strike me as worthy of canonization. No child should be subjected to such horrific imagery and I find it difficult to fathom the mind of someone who is prepared to invest such total degradation on a fellow human being. Vengeance was being exacted on innocents, on women and children who knew nothing of the political machinations that were being wielded, which in turn were to scar, if not end, their lives.

I stare into the pool of golden nectar. The hymns from the faithful inside the main temple, the Harimandir Sahib, lilt gently across the balmy air. I am suddenly struck by how calm and peaceful this place is, a genuine sanctuary for reflection. Given that Sikhs were renowned warriors, the underlying philosophy of the faith is of total peace and the Golden Temple underlines that. As does Mr BB Singh himself, a fine advertisement for Sikhism, and indeed humanity itself.

The remnants of Mr Singh's family ultimately made it across the border to rebuild their lives, much as my family did. Now it was time for me to cross that same border, but in the direction that millions of Muslims, uprooted and suffering violent retribution, were also forced to take. Mr Singh found peace and closure on his journey back in time. What would I find? Well, I was about to find out.

PART FOUR

BACK TO THE FUTURE

CHAPTER TEN

Onward to the Past

With BB Singh's horrific ordeal burned on to my retinas, I had an uncomfortable night. I found it impossible to disassociate that level of terror from all the elderly, kind, smiling faces of my aunts, uncles and, before them, my grandparents. They, my parents and their friends had never even hinted at the physical and emotional turmoil they must have encountered and endured in those dreadful times. Time to move on to the border … and the past.

The border on the only main road between India and Pakistan lies at a small crossing called Wagah. The thirty-minute journey from Amritsar finds us flanked by the lush agricultural land that Punjab is so famous for. The road is fairly empty with the odd car, bus or tractor passing by and the drivers letting us know they exist by tooting their horns. As I gaze at this placid scene, I can't help seeing the ghosts of all those millions of families from sixty years ago, carrying everything they now owned, on this very road. Both streams of people, heading in opposite directions, were at times just a few hundred yards apart. Desperation, frustration and at times unadulterated hatred would often spill over and violent conflict would spark up. Colonial army units had begun to pull out before the Independence deadline of 15 August 1947, and the two foetal nations had neither the time nor the resource to police such an exodus.

OPPOSITE: The Badshahi Mosque, Lahore.

ABOVE: Crossing the border. The border guard stifles laughter as he peruses my passport photo. Relieved, I take my first steps in the Islamic Republic of Pakistan.

We pull into the Wagah border area quite suddenly. A modest customs and immigration hall awaits us and we start the laborious task of having our media equipment checked and stamped. As I wander back out to look at the road running into Pakistan, I see a flurry of activity and follow the melée. Porters carrying boxes of fruit and what look like duvets are rushing towards the border where, in single file, they hand over their consignments to their Pakistani counterparts. Evidently, trucks are seen as a security risk and so all goods are portered in the old-fashioned way. There is a modest monument on the Indian side of the border, two hands clasped in a handshake. Underneath is a caption that reads: 'Dedicated to 10 Lakh Punjabis that died unsung in 1947'. That's one million dead, dear reader.

Our camera gear having been verified, our crew collect together to make sure we're all here and we've got our passports and all-important visas. I double-check that I have my dad's memory map. The tall, handsome border security officer checks our papers and we cross the historic Line of Partition. I feel slightly dazed, as I become the first member of my family to walk on Pakistani soil for sixty years.

As I take my first faltering steps I hear a voice shout out, 'Mr Kumar! Welcome to Pakistan!', a reference to a character I have played on television. I wave and shout a thank you. I can feel myself welling up; a Pakistani Muslim is welcoming a British Hindu into his country from India. Surreal? Totally. Progress? Maybe. Hope? Definitely.

After Pakistani official formalities have been completed, we're introduced to our local fixer named Khalid. He'll be with us for the duration of our short stay in Pakistan, having organized our filming permits. We board our vans and head for Gujranwala and Badhoki Gosaiyan, on our ever-present friend, the Grand Trunk Road.

Khalid is a tall, moustachioed chatty man with a smile in his voice, and he seems to be dressed in Pashtun-style clothes: long beige *kameez* shirt, matching *salwar* pyjama bottoms and small hat that is so immoveable that I wonder whether it's actually part of his head. Unsurprisingly, Khalid tells me he hails from the North West Frontier region of Pakistan. The local scenery doesn't look drastically different to the other side of the fence, so to speak, but the small dwellings that appear from time to time look relatively dilapidated. After about twenty minutes we pass through our first built-up area, on the outskirts of Lahore's suburbs. It seems poor and disorganized, a bit like the small towns I encountered on bus journeys in India thirty years ago. The people look poorer too, a stark contrast to the inhabitants of the suburbs of Amritsar, equidistant on the other side of the divide. It also seems odd to be in a place that seems familiar, but where I can't read any of the hoardings or shop names, as they're almost all in Urdu script.

'Hey, look at those oranges!' Andy, our sound recordist, points out in his easy American drawl. Sure enough, there are piles of luscious oranges stacked up on wooden hand carts. They look perfect, down to a little green leaf protruding from a stem. Cezanne would have trodden on his palette in excitement by now.

BELOW: Simple monument on the Indian side of the border, honouring one million Punjabis who died in 1947.

Khalid brings our minibus to a halt and with all the grace of a mountain goat leaps out, purchases a dozen of these large beauties and we're all devouring them before anyone can say 'hesperidium'. Our vehicle is now consumed by slurping and lip-smacking sounds; no one can believe just how delicious these oranges are.

'These are amazing, Khalid!' I splutter.

'Oh, yes,' he replies. 'This region is famous across Pakistan for the oranges.'

'Wow! What is it? Something in the soil or preparation?' I ask him.

DEDICATED TO
10 LAKH PUNJABIS
WHO DIED UNSUNG
IN 1947

'Genetic modification,' says Khalid, smiling proudly.

We reach Lahore, capital of the Punjab region and the second largest city in Pakistan. Papaji, my uncle in Karnal, studied here and this was where my father-in-law was born, and a friend's father worked in the law courts. It was always known as a city of culture and learning stretching back to Mughal times and it's still seen as Pakistan's trendiest city. Lahore is home to fashion shows, Pakistan's small film industry and one of South Asia's most popular rock bands, called Junoon. Unfortunately we don't have time to see the sights, but Khalid shouts out landmarks as we pass them.

'University of Punjab on the right.'

We drive past the huge impressive colonial building where Papaji studied in the early 1940s. It is the oldest and largest university in Pakistan.

'Anarkali bazaar, right next to it,' sings Khalid.

I see, fleetingly, the entrance to one of the most renowned markets in the subcontinent, which dates back over 200 years. It's frustrating not to be able to stop and take in the history, but Gujranwala is still a couple of hours away and we still have to locate the village of Badhoki. The centre of Lahore appears spacious, with great care having been taken not to crowd the many Mughal and British Raj-era buildings. There also seems to be a large number of well-maintained parks.

We finally stop in one for a spot of lunch. Khalid has a mini picnic prepared of sandwiches, crisps and mini juice cartons. Not quite the local cuisine we were hoping for. I look around this unnamed, mani-cured patch of green; grass, hedges, benches, flowers and a few trees. Nothing unusual and little sign here of this being an Islamic republic, save for the fact there seem to be fewer women about.

Khalid tells me that there are still restrictions on Indians and Pakistanis travelling in each other's country, but tensions have eased since the last armed conflict between India and Pakistan – the three-month Kargil conflict over Kashmir in 1999. Today there is a visa quota for cricket fans and pilgrimages. However, visas are only issued on the

OPPOSITE: Many of Pakistan's mosques were built at the height of the Mughal empire, showing its distinctive architectural influence.

permission of visiting specified areas. Khalid has never been to India and hopes to visit some day. I like him. He's open, honest and is funnier than he knows or perhaps intends.

'My brother lives in Australia. Married an Australian girl; they got three little kangaroos.' He smiles. 'But when he come home, he wants to sleep with his mother; always sleeping with the mother. Imagine a grown man sleeping with his mother!'

With suppressed smiles the crew avoid eye contact with each other. We know he means it innocently, no one mentions Oedipus and this seems an opportune time to move on.

We leave the outskirts of Lahore and rejoin the GT Road heading north towards Gujranwala, birthplace of both my parents. I'm heady with excitement, reading and rereading my father's map and reviewing the small details with Khalid. Is the old railway station still there? That was where my grandfather had his day job, working on this small section of the mammoth railway network the British bequeathed to the two new nations. He never got to see the new India, passing away a couple of years beforehand, but mercifully he never got to see the carnage either.

Within a couple of hours we reach the industrial city of Gujranwala, a sort of Sheffield or Detroit equivalent. Apparently it was renowned for two things in particular – stainless steel and, according to my dad, wrestlers. Almost on cue, a mule cart clanks by laden with stainless steel plates. I wait momentarily for someone to randomly get someone else into a half nelson but it doesn't happen. My father's

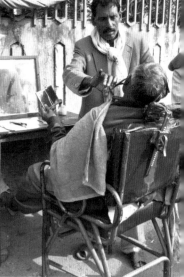

house was close to the GT Road, and one of the landmarks my father has illustrated is the 'Sialkot Gate'. We almost pass it completely until Khalid points it out. The gate itself is now embedded in a narrow lane with shops and buildings, the latter built so haphazardly that the gate is almost totally obscured from the GT Road running past it. The main thoroughfare is crowded and chaotic. Buildings, billboards, high-tension cables and a flyover give a sense of anarchy above, and at street level, our minibus is caught up in the usual bedlam of motor vehicles, horse-drawn carts, bicycles and pedestrians.

As we sit in the crowded traffic, I am presented with a bombshell that leaves me speechless. A production oversight means that we cannot film here in Gujranwala, as we have neither the time nor the necessary permissions. I'm gutted. I can't believe that I've come this far with my dad's map and that we are going to pass straight through it. We're only allowed to film at my father's ancestral village. This of course can happen, particularly on a big shoot, entailing months of filming and planning – a hotel is forgotten to be booked, a story is overlooked, a flight is missed and a date misread. But on the most personal journey of any programme I've made, I find it very hard to be upbeat and jovial.

Khalid quietly ushers the driver onward through the polluted throng as I sit silently trying to come to terms with this cruel twist. We drive on in a silence made of granite. I now have to focus on other landmarks my dad's map gives me, leading me to Badhoki. One end of the rainbow with its pot of gold fades behind me as I consign my anger

ABOVE: Street scenes of the GT Road, Pakistan. (left) A boy sits by a typically painted truck, just outside Lahore. (right) A roadside barber – not a lot of styles to choose from, it seems.

217

and tears to the 'to be dealt with later' file in my head and try to work out which turning we need to take from the GT Road. After about forty minutes and stopping a couple of times to ask some folk for directions, we see the turning.

Badhoki Gosaiyan was a small village consisting of about forty homes and surrounded by agricultural lands back in 1947. The road turning left off the GTR is not much more than a dirt track, and apart from an unattractive sub power station running alongside it, I can't imagine it would have looked radically different back then.

My dad's biro flourishes indicate a *gurdwara*, a Sikh temple, on the right-hand side of the road surrounded by a large, deep watertank. According to my dad, the temple was built almost 500 years ago. Incredibly, it's still there. It looks in slight disrepair and the water is long gone, but it's huge, appearing to be about the size of half a football field and possibly 15 feet deep (there are boys playing cricket in there, giving some indication of its size). This is the first physical evidence of how good my dad's memory is. But can we find the house?

We pass through the tiny village and park outside the village school. Villagers slowly emerge and congregate, watching this odd scene: two minibuses, a white camera crew, some other strangers and a guy wearing an Afghan-style hat that doesn't move at all on his head. The villagers nudge each other and point like they're watching a deft circus act. There probably hasn't been this much excitement here since 1947.

'Right!' intones Khalid loudly to the burgeoning crowd, in Urdu. 'Does anyone know of a large building with twenty-foot high gates?' No response. 'Any houses left from 1947?'

'I know where there's one.' A youngish man yells, his confidence waning through his sentence.

'Go on then,' yells Khalid as we all move off like a swarm, villagers in tow.

More and more locals join the treasure hunt, as we wend this way and that. My father had explained that the ancestral home was the largest building in the village, built at the highest elevation and had very tall, large wooden gates preceding a courtyard. All the inhabitants today originally came from India, and some tell me that there are only about six original *hawelis* (large residential villas) left in Badhoki. The streets are narrow and I notice that the bricks used in some of the houses are very thin, indicating that they are the oldest structures. The whole scene is very medieval in feel.

As we duck in and out of alleys we pick up quite an entourage, as news of these foreigners with cameras filters swiftly through the tiny locale. Khalid had warned me that the older generation, those that made the exodus from India, may give me a hard time about being Indian, as they would remember the terrible ordeal at first hand, but the younger generation would be absolutely fine. I steel myself as a few men older than my dad join the procession. However, they too are more caught up in the torrent of the hunt than in any apparent misgivings about having an Indian in their midst. I don't have time to savour the fact that I'm in

BELOW: Lahore's Badshahi Mosque, commissioned by the Mughal Emperor Aurangzeb, bears a striking resemblance to the Jama Masjid in Delhi, which was built, as it happens, by Aurangzeb's father, the Emperor Shah Jahan.

my father's village at all, as we frenetically reach a *haweli*, eliminate it from our list and move on to the next one.

But no one can recall my dad's landmarks: a large house with massive wooden gates with a well situated behind it. Strangers allow us to enter their homes and climb to the roofs to somehow locate any other land-marks. On the roof of one house, I take a moment to look around. The village is still small and surrounded by open fields, and in my mind I catch a glimpse of my father as a little child running amok in the constricted lanes suddenly bursting out into wide unadulterated space.

Then something catches my eye – the tallest building in the village. It's a mosque, its tall minaret glinting slightly in the late afternoon light. A local chap, Mushtaq, tells me that the mosque was built about forty years ago … on the highest part of the village. All my senses screech to a halt. That's where my father's house would have been. It's gone. I have mixed feelings at this point. On the one hand, I've made it to the village of one half of my heritage, but on the other, I can't really step foot into the rooms where my dad spent so much time as a boy.

Our work here is done and the last of the sun's rays is waving a benign farewell. I can't help thinking about the missed opportunities in this part of my journey: not being able to stop in Gujranwala, not having enough time to explore Lahore and not finding the house in Badhoki. But I'm here. I've had a chance to step through a time portal and, even briefly, managed a glance at my father's childhood.

As we head back towards the minibuses, Mushtaq approaches me and asks me in Punjabi, 'What is this film you're making here, exactly?'

'Well, I'm retracing my father's steps across Partition,' I tell him. 'This was his village and I just wanted to see it.'

'What a wonderful thing you are doing, giving your father such respect. It's important to know one's roots, isn't it?'

I agree with him. 'Everyone should know their roots and respect everyone else's too.'

'Yes,' says Mushtaq. He pauses. 'Next time you come please bring your father too. We'll have tea together … this is his village too.'

Once again, I have to stifle back tears as I thank him for his generosity. I also feel a resolve rising up within me. No more mixed feelings, this journey was worth every hopeful, annoying, joyous frustrating minute.

I have one final task to perform before I leave. I ring my dad back in London.

'Hi, Dad, guess where I'm calling from … Badhoki Gosaiyan … yes, near a school … it was there when you were a kid? No, the house isn't there anymore, only a few buildings from that time still exist, but the *gurdwara* is still there … yes, so is the tank but no water in it … no, we can't film in Gujranwala … I'll tell you about it when I get back … hello? Hello?' The signal had gone.

We bid farewell to my forefathers' village and head back on to the GT Road towards Lahore.

ABOVE: Phoning my dad from the village he hasn't seen for over 60 years. I became a witness to his childhood.

Quick stop and snoop

As we once again prepare to drive through Gujranwala I feel an urgency to stop. We needed to get to the border before it closed but I just couldn't let this moment pass. I was here, I had a map and I was going to use it, dammit! If I couldn't find the place my dad was born, maybe I could find the house where he grew up. We did not have permission to film here, but surely we could get away with a quick stop and snoop.

We parked up just off the GT Road and I asked Deep the producer and the ever-reliable Khalid to accompany me as I determine to find my dad's town house. His recollection of Gujranwala is more acute than the village and the map is relatively detailed. We cross the now disused rail line next to the main road. My father had marked out a short cut he used to take past a temple and, miraculously, both are still there after sixty years. His house was next to his school but I can find no markers for either of these. We knock at a door randomly and an elderly gentleman emerges.

'Sorry to disturb you,' I tell him in Punjabi, 'I'm looking for an old school that used to be here.'

'Why?'

'Well, my father attended it, when he was a child.'

'What was it called?' he asks.

I'm dreading this question, as it will in part give away my identity to a man who's of the right age to despise me.

'King George Hindu High School.' I tell him, awaiting the onslaught.

'Are you from India?'

'Well, I live in London, but yes my parents went to India in 1947.'

'I came the other way,' he tells me, 'from Ambala.'

'That's not far from Karnal, where my mother's family went,' I say.

'I went to Karnal once, when I was really little,' he adds.

He tells me that his house, the one he still lives in, once belonged to a Hindu woman but that's all he knows. He summons two small boys and tells them to take me to the school. Before I leave he says, 'Do you have time for a cup of tea?'

A small innocuous question that says so much. I thank him and tell him not this time.

The two boys take me and Deep through some winding streets to an alley that gets narrower and darker as we move along it. Finally it's so dark that I cannot see the walls either side of me and have to continually touch them to guide me.

'This is it, we're here,' says one of the boys. I close my eyes and count to ten in order to adjust them to the gloom. When I open them, I can faintly make out the walls either side of me and the alley in front of me disappearing around the corner.

'How do you know the school was here?' I ask the boys. They simply extend their index fingers and point upwards. I realize why it had suddenly got so dark. Above me is an enormous vaulted wooden roof, covering the entire area. A voice behind me makes me jump.

'That's the old school roof,' says a man who had silently joined the team. 'Kashmiri refugees settled here first and then built houses, two storeys high some of them, all under the roof … it gets quite hot in the summer though.'

I know my father's house faced the old school, so working my way back to the service road that was on the map I tried to find the closest single-storey building facing it. There wasn't one there. New domiciles had sprung up over the last sixty years, unsurprisingly, but heck: I'd found the old school he went to. This was the same school where Papaji had told me about the three men who'd survived the young mobs intent on killing them. These were the streets where my dad had played cricket, and I'd even walked the short cut he would take to the station.

As Deep and I walked back to the waiting crew in the vans, I was once again filled with emotion. The tragedy of these innocent streets that later ran with blood, and then became home to the pained and dispossessed. What a waste.

I was, and still am, irked and frustrated that I didn't have the opportunity of spending more time in Gujranwala, and that we don't have a filmed document of it. But once again the much bigger picture is that I became a witness to my parents' childhood and have trodden at least some of their steps. And in my small quest I met still innocent people with generosity, love and humanity in their hearts.

We reach the Wagah border just in time for the daily closing ceremony at dusk and the regular large crowd has already arrived. Grandstand seats on both sides give spectators a view of a theatrical show of machismo and nationalistic showboating. As we present our papers and step back on to Indian soil, I notice that the Pakistani seating is segregated by gender. Men are waving the green and crescent-moon flags and one particular stalwart is wearing a totally green outfit with the flag knitted into his sweatshirt. He takes to holding two flags and running up to the gates and waving them furiously as the crowd cheers him on.

On the Indian side are a couple of thousand patriots waving flags and taking photos. Here, random individuals are waving India's tricolour at the gates, though this time, as if to make a point, a number of women, some of them elderly, take the role of standard bearers.

I take up a position on the Indian side and a man asks me if I want a beer. Freedom indeed. I politely decline and settle in to watch the proceedings. The Indians who are *bhangra* dancing like they're at a wedding are ushered back to their seats and the evening's display begins. Soldiers from both sides stamp their feet and indulge in high kicking in a coordinated display of preening ritual. They pull stern faces and eyeball each other across the open border gate in a display of mock aggression and intimidation. All the while being cheered by their respective fans.

This is certainly not what I expected. The atmosphere is a strange mix of Broadway musical, football match and family function. The Indians chant 'Hindustan ki Jai' (Praise to Hindustan), while their opposite numbers shout 'Pakistan Zindabad' (Pakistan Forever). At the appointed moment both flags are lowered simultaneously so no one's flag has ascendancy, and a brief handshake between two of the soldiers marks the end of the day. The gates on both sides are closed till morning.

As the people file out, there are waves and smiles to the departees on the other side of the gate. Are these people really so divided?

As I amble back to our minibuses I notice two signs, designed to inform those entering from Pakistan. One says 'India, the world's largest democracy welcomes you'. The other is a stylized emblem comprising Muslim, Sikh, Hindu and Christian symbols.

As we head back down the GT Road again, I try to make some sense of this part of my adventure. My heart aches for all those dispossessed, particularly since it seems so needless. A generation was decimated and traumatized, and for what? The tragedy didn't lead to anyone getting more land, resources, religious sites or economic or strategic advantage – the usual reasons for war. It can be argued that the lives of the majority were not better off because of it. No one gained morality or pride over it and it didn't alter the border either. And there were the more lasting effects beyond the horrific violence and deaths in August 1947.

Partition didn't just end at the physical border. People were partitioned; their hearts and minds were partitioned. A contrived enmity was created which lasts overtly to this day. But covertly, the people in this area, who speak the same language and who had up until sixty years ago

BELOW: Auditioning for the Rockettes?

coexisted for hundreds of years, have no such hatred. They see each other as two sides of the same coin. To hate one side is to hate yourself.

I thought again about the incredible journey that my parents and people like them made. Not only violently uprooted from everything they ever knew and moved as refugees to a new land, but then, as a direct result of having nothing, to restart … again, by making the pioneering trip to a cold small island on the other side of the world for a better life in Britain – the land of their former oppressors. I think about how many of those educated, diligent folk arrived in Britain where their qualifications were meaningless and they had to make do with working in factories, on buses and trains and opening up newspaper shops at 5 in the morning. And I think about the mistrust and dismissive attitude they received in those early years (and receive to this day in some parts of the country), and this after everything they'd been through.

Some of that generation is thankfully still with us. So next time you buy a newspaper, or have your ticket checked at the station or haggle with an old Indian cab driver, just take a moment to think about the journey that person has been on. They may have faced nightmares we wouldn't dare to speak of.

CHAPTER ELEVEN

Barefoot Maharajahs, Hold the Mayo

After my emotionally exhausting voyage round my father's past, I'm hoping for sights and sounds to delight the senses. The aged aeroplane's engines scream and the overhead luggage compartments rattle as we finally touch down in Jodhpur, one of the most picturesque cities in the western state of Rajasthan, on this, the last leg of our journey. As we slowly taxi towards Jodhpur's terminal building, the unmistakable sound of Lionel Richie being played on a Bontempi organ comes back to haunt me. Muzak, Indian style.

Rajasthan, or 'Land of Kings', has long been considered one of India's most beautiful and historic states. It is India's largest state and has a population about the size of Britain's and I have had occasion to visit it before. The last time I was in Rajasthan was about seven years ago, though my sense memory of it is not a positive one. I had gone to Jaipur, the capital city and on my first evening had been taken to a little local restaurant. Even though I had determined to be a vegetarian for at least a week while in India, I was persuaded into trying a chicken biriyani, 'the best in Jaipur' I was told. By ten o'clock that night I was exploding through every orifice and by midnight I was dry heaving. I should add that India was in the middle of a heatwave and it was 90

OPPOSITE:
Cuckoo, cuckoo. At the mighty Mehrangarh Fort.

degrees through the night. At one in the morning the electricity went and there was no air conditioning and no fan. By three, I'd decided that my 48 hours in India was more than I could handle and resolved that I would take the first plane back to London so I could die there. Of course, after another 24 hours following continual doses of rehydration salts and soup, I felt well enough to continue, but the feeling that Rajasthan was more than I could handle had never entirely gone away. This time I'd already been to a variety of out-of-the-way places and was older and wiser, so perhaps I would conquer any bug the land of kings had to offer.

As the plane manoeuvres to its final stop, I can see numerous empty aircraft bunkers – fighter planes buzz and dart overhead like wasps, and here on the runway moustachioed army officers attempt to look busy in the winter sun. With its proximity to Pakistan, Jodhpur has always been a crucial military base; the town was built around the fifteenth-century fort that rises from its heart, the last great Indian citadel before the dusty plains of Rajasthan give way to the great Thar Desert.

I've come to Jodhpur for several reasons. OK, so it's a beautiful place to stop on my homeward-bound trajectory and I'm hardly complaining, but also I've been invited to the Maharajah's birthday celebrations. I've always been intrigued by the maharajahs of India but my exposure to them has been largely through movies and literature. They were normally depicted as large fat men in bejewelled turbans sitting on an oversized set of scales, while peasants poured precious gemstones on the opposite tray, hoping it would balance out, else they would be fed to the royal tigers. More rarely they would be warrior heroes who fought against the mighty Mughal Empire. Colonial photographs showed them as British wannabes who posed with visiting British dignitaries, one foot courageously resting on a tiger that had met its end when faced by twenty guns after being chased to exhaustion.

None of the modern images had brought them much dignity and I wonder whether these hereditary leaders are still relevant in twenty-first-century India. But before I pass judgement perhaps I ought to

actually meet one, and this one has been kind enough to even send me an invitation card.

'HRH Raj Rajeshwar Saramad-i-Rajha-i-Hindustan Maharajad-hiraja Maharajah Shri GAJ SINGHJI II Sahib Bahadur Singh requests the pleasure of' etc., etc. … Gosh, what do we sing when we get to 'Happy Birthday dear …?'

At the palace gates, I emerge from my car and am received by a man with a truly magnificent moustache. It extends across most of his face, and yet is not a beard. It is a moustache that would make Dali feel ridiculous, as if he needed the help. No, the palace attendants at Umaid-Bahwan, city residence of the Maharajah of Jodhpur, have moustaches that would make big cats cower.

This particularly well-coiffed chap leads me through an art deco hallway into a circular central lobby of such stupendous opulence that one subconsciously begins to whisper as soon as one enters its embrace. Cool, pale marble reflects brass and candlelight. Stuffed leopards and tigers peer down from the walls, making me feel ever-more inadequate.

It's worth bearing in mind that palaces like Umaid-Bahwan were built for this very reason; not so much to provide warmth and comfort as to provoke awe and due deference. This particular building, with its art deco tiles and looming staircases has the distinctively authoritarian air of the 1930s, like an angular and slightly neo-fascist version of Washington's Capitol building, and is reminiscent of the Lutyens architecture in New Delhi.

Umaid-Bahwan was first commissioned by Maharajah Umaid Singh in 1929, and as was all the rage amongst the Indian princes of the era, he engaged a British architect, H.V. Lanchester, to oversee his grand design. A severe drought in the area at the time had laid much of the local workforce to waste and the Maharajah brought employment to almost 5,000 local builders, taking them more than 15 years to build the astonishing edifice. Thirsty work I would say.

There is no concrete or mortar used to construct the mainframe of the palace, simply a series of interlocking stones. The result is breathtaking. It was the largest private residence in the world at one time, but the present Maharajah was prescient in turning part of it into a luxury hotel in the 1970s.

I follow the palace attendant across the lobby, and just as my eyes have become accustomed to the vast and subdued atrium, we emerge blinking into the sunlight. A hundred red-carpeted steps below us, a garden party is in full swing.

I consider for a moment walking down the red carpet – after all I've done it loads of times at movie premieres, but then I've never had to contend with pike bearers in Leicester Square. I decide to walk next to the red carpet, striding wilfully past the hotel's paying guests, who are confined to the terrace and can only gaze forlornly at the real guests on the lawn below. The sequins of countless saris glint in the blazing winter sun, and the waxed handlebars of a hundred moustaches twitch as I begin to mingle with Jodhpur's great, good and just plain lucky.

The brass band strikes up to announce the arrival of their Majesties. The music is, like so much in Rajasthan, almost beyond description. The overall barrage of sound is a marriage of the strident brass of a Scottish marching band with the wailing clarinet and pounding bass drum all too familiar to those who have ever attended an Indian wedding.

In any case, the Maharajah is clearly taking it all in his stride as he and the Maharani sashay down their red carpet, the pike bearers snapping to attention as they pass. The well-wishers down below applaud respectfully but as soon as the royal feet touch the royal lawn a scrum ensues. Cameras jostle for position in a disorderly tangle of limbs, gifts and moustaches.

The King and Queen are festooned with flower garlands, which they politely remove and pass to their bearers only to have them instantly replaced by the next guest who has managed to force their way to the front of the unruly crowd. Guests assemble to present their offerings and the central tenets of Indian road sense are applied: every man for himself, and see a gap and go for it. I've brought flowers with

OPPOSITE: Jodhpur – the Blue City, as beautiful as an Impressionist painting.

me, but looking around, three hundred other guests have thought the same thing. After being jostled continuously to the back of the queue like the smallest kid at a free ice-cream sale, I finally decide to go native, stick my elbows out and move forward like a Panzer tank. The one edge I have over my bouqueted competitors is that my offering is a good two feet higher than anyone else's. That's class that is.

Three places in front of me, two men present their beautifully wrapped gift, but rather than merely hand it over, they insist on unwrapping it before the Maharajah. I wait for the music to stop so that it can be passed on and some else can start furiously unwrapping it. Finally liberated from its sparkling paper prison, what is revealed is a rather crap painting; so lousy in fact that my 14-month-old son could have done it. The Maharajah nods and smiles appreciatively and accepts it in the spirit in which it was given. If I'd been receiving it, it would have been in a charity shop before the sun had set. Throughout it all, the Royals remain patient and gracious and I get the feeling that they genuinely have love and respect for their subjects.

Finally, it's my turn:

'Your Royal Highness, may I, on behalf of myself and the crew, present this small token of our gratitude and wish you a happy birthday.'

'Thank you and welcome, lovely to see you,' replies the King.

'And I didn't get it from duty free either,' I blunder.

'Oh!' says the Maharani. 'How wonderful to meet you. I watch you on TV all the time.'

BELOW: (left) At the Maharajah's palace, not being tempted by the red carpet. (right) Traditional Rajasthani puppets.

This has me totally flummoxed. The last thing I expected was to be recognized by people who can trace their family tree back 700 years.

'Thank you, I'm speechless!' I splutter. With a swift glance behind me, I see some in line looking enquiringly at the stranger that the Royals are expending their precious time on; others are looking dejectedly at their newly inadequate floral tributes.

I move aside, basking in the attention slightly and the disorganized throng resume their focus on the birthday boy. This Maharajah is unlike all those caricatured ones I've seen in photographs and movies; he's warm and engaging with a public-school clipped English accent, and moves effortlessly into Hindi and Marwari, the local Rajasthani dialect.

The celebrations too are modest. No elephants, camels or trays of diamonds and rubies here. There's a buffet, tea and coffee and, most disarmingly, even a birthday cake. It feels very much like a normal family occasion, apart from the awesome backdrop of the imposing palace behind. One of the guests, a lady so well endowed that I constantly waited for her to topple over (fortunately, her enormous feet nullified that), tells me that this is his private celebration – the public event contains the pomp and circumstance that the people expect, but she's reluctant to divulge whether elephants and camels are involved, though the trays of diamonds and rubies are ruled right out.

The guests are an interesting mix: local dignitaries, neighbouring Royal Princes, business associates and the Prince and Princess of Jodhpur's pals. A lucky few seem to be just normal folk who behave

BELOW: (left) The King and Queen of Cool: down-to-earth, great sense of humour and genuine humility of their position and duties. (right) 'You're not allowed in here, sonny.'

like they've won a competition. To emphasize the private and modest nature of the celebration, there are even friends of the Maharajah from his Oxford University days. Watching him joke and reminisce with them makes me forget momentarily that he's the symbolic head of a kingdom – he could be a don or successful businessman simply chatting to his mates.

The Maharani is an attractive, vivacious lady who introduces me to other guests and asks me how the rest of the cast of *The Kumars at Number 42* are.

'Well, I think they're fine, I haven't spoken to Vincent and Indira who play my parents since I've been in India, but Meera who plays my grandmother is very well. I spoke to her last night, actually.'

'Really?' asks the Maharani. 'How come?'

'Well, you did know she's my wife?' I ask, sensing a misunderstanding looming

The Maharani's eyes narrowed and her brow furrowed slightly. 'You married that old lady?' she said slowly, with just a modicum of dignified disgust.

'No, no, it's make-up, it's a young lady in make-up.' A random female voice shouted. There was palpable relief on all sides before the Maharani was whisked away to meet some important people. I was left feeling grateful that she wasn't hauled away before the awful image in her head had been erased.

Apart from the brass band that seem to explode haphazardly into discordant yet entertaining life, there is a visiting British theatre company that has been roped into singing a couple of numbers. It's not what they normally do I know, but I watch inscrutably as they murder 'Fever' before moving on to brutalize various classics by the Beatles. The proceedings come to an end with a selected few surrounding the cake and singing 'Happy Birthday' (incidentally it was 'Happy Birthday dear Bapji …'), with the nice Royal personage even handing me a piece of cake.

As the remnants begin to leave I finally get the chance to walk the

OPPOSITE: Traditionally, it was high caste Hindu homes that were painted blue, giving Jodhpur its nickname of the 'Blue City'.

red carpet, accompanying the Maharani, pike bearers standing to attention as we pass. Cool.

Early the next morning I have an appointment with the Maharajah as he checks up on some of the conservation projects he supports locally. We set out from the palace in a very modern but utilitarian 4x4. It's comfortable of course, but not at all flashy or showy; the interior is even denied the tinsel and bunting so beloved of Indians the world over. There isn't even a gilded tissue box on the back shelf. The Maharajah is dressed casually in white with a sombre waistcoat, with the traditional Rajasthani turban providing a flash of colour. As we drive across the endless dusty landscape, he points out that in a region where it only rains three months a year, it's absolutely essential to make the best use of Rajasthan's most precious commodity – water. He now spends much of his time trying to reinforce the traditional methods people had of conserving the water – looking after the village ponds, tanks, keeping the water clean.

The Maharajah (known locally as Bapji or Respected Father) was born in 1948 just a few months after India was reborn as an independent republic, and life appears to have changed drastically for the royals of Rajasthan since the heady days of the Raj. Under British rule, the numerous royal families of India were feted and in return for their compliance, cooperation and on occasions their unconditional support, they were allowed to keep a degree of governance over their kingdoms and some influence in their people's affairs. The various principalities had never had any sense of a unified India – before the British there had been no country known as India. It was simply a region that stretched out towards Burma in the east and Afghanistan in the west. The Maharajahs of India had been involved in guerrilla warfare against the Mughals for centuries, but under the British, they had a period of consistency and establishment.

After Independence, however, and now subsumed within the modern nation of India, they were given a stipend from the government and though stripped of political and administrative power, they were allowed to continue living and maintaining their palaces. They had no tax-raising powers now, and thus began their decline. This was hastened when the government systematically withdrew the privy purses from all of India's royal families during the late 1960s and early 1970s. This led many of them into financial ruin, but the smarter ones adapted, moving into commerce, politics, tourism and social work aimed at their community.

As we travelled in modest comfort in the air-conditioned royal vehicle, I asked the Maharajah about the moment that he realized that he had a job to do.

'Probably when I came back here after graduating from Oxford in 1970. The welcome I received after being away for so long pursuing my studies abroad was so tremendous, so warm, that I properly realized that there was a profound connection between myself and the people. That's when I fully committed myself to doing whatever I could to help.'

BELOW: Villagers in their finery are still drawn to the major cities to make a living for themselves. Despite this, most of India's population is still firmly rural.

As we approach a small village, the familiar sound of drums and song resonates through the air and an impressive group of sari-clad and brightly coloured turbaned villagers wait to greet him.

'I think they know you're here,' I tell his Highness.

A group of a hundred workers gather to hear the Maharajah's encouraging words, and as an honoured guest, I'm presented with a traditional turban and garland of flowers.

The Maharajah whispers that the reception we are given today is typical of most villages he visits, and that he often tries to tone down the rapturous welcome he receives. However, as he rightly points out, in India any excuse for a celebration is enthusiastically taken.

After some serious fawning by villagers has taken place and a couple of cups of tea (and a biscuit) have been consumed, we put our hands together in a *namaste* and take our leave. As the car leaves the farewell drums and singing behind I ask the Maharajah,

'Has public perception of you as Maharajah changed over the years?'

'We don't have power anymore, but we have some influence,' he replies matter-of-factly. 'And it's important that we use whatever influence we have to better the condition of our people. The bond between my family and the local community goes back hundreds of years; unlike politicians who frequently move from area to area in pursuit of their careers or if unelected return to private business, I am connected with these people and this earth ... thus the people know that we're not going anywhere.'

The car stops momentarily to allow a goat herder to pass with his flock. An old man suddenly recognizes the King, approaches and in a cyclone of thanks exhausts himself before asking if 'Bapji' would come round for tea? Bapji warmly acknowledges the compliments and tells him that he's busy right now.

'He's older so has some decorum. Some of the younger ones, and particularly tourists, just barge in, sometimes without asking and quickly take a photo,' says the Maharajah, barging me playfully.

'How do you feel about this new celebrity status?' I ask.

Bapji laughs. 'It doesn't detract from what's important and that's the welfare of the people. Anyway, we all have to move with the times.'

We visit several water harvesting projects. 'The most important commodity in Rajasthan is water,' Bapji reiterates. Large collecting tanks on a school involve the students and ancient tanks constructed several hundred years ago are shored up and involve the surrounding villages. Here, the empowerment of women is also an issue and women are formed into cooperatives to look after and administer some of the schemes.

Everywhere we go, the Maharajah is greeted warmly and tourists and visiting university students edge in for a photo opportunity. The concept of celebrity wouldn't have made much sense to the Maharajah's mighty ancestors, whose fame came from fighting big bloody battles and building bloody big forts. Bapji promised to show me the centre-piece of his kingdom.

Mehrangarh Fort, around which the city of Jodhpur is built, is one of the biggest of his ancestors' big forts. After a change of cars to a far more town-friendly saloon, we take the only road up to the medieval fort. It slowly comes into view like the sun emerging from an eclipse. The sheer scale alone forces a sharp intake of breath followed by a whispered expletive from me. Either no one noticed or they must be used to that kind of response by now. This huge structure sits atop a huge hill and seems almost as wide as it is tall, eliciting shock and awe before any futile thoughts of taking it. It looks like something from one of the *Lord of the Rings* movies, rising up like a titan dominating the area around it. Guards salute as we drive beyond the public car park and into the fort itself. Once, its survival was based on keeping people out, but the Maharajah has found that the only way he can preserve it today is by letting the tourists in.

The citadel was built in 1459 by Rao Jodha (after whom Jodhpur was named) and the city gradually evolved around it. There are some wonderful stories surrounding this magnificent structure, including the burial of a man alive within the walls. According to folklore, the

OVERLEAF: Mehrangarh Fort. Like an unreal Hollywood set.

construction of Mehrangarh on top of this rocky 400-foot hill forced a hermit named Cheeria Nathji to abandon his cave. This provoked him to curse both Jodha and his city. Un-nerved by this curse, Jodha took an extreme measure to appease the Gods. I ask the Maharajah about this as I accompany him around the fortress.

'Bapji, is it true that there was a human sacrifice, when the fort was being built? I heard a man was buried alive in its foundations?'

'Yes. A volunteer was asked for and a man stepped forward and presented himself. The Maharajah of the time promised that the man's family and his descendants would be looked after by the Royal Family.'

'So does that mean to this day? His descendants are still looked after?'

'Oh yes. In fact one of that man's family works here at the fort.'

I thought about this for a second. 'Boy, I bet he's hoping you're not going to build an extension.'

Climbing some stairs to a modestly sized courtyard, Bapji shows me the tiny ceremonial marble throne, upon which he was crowned. He became the Maharajah at the impossibly young age of four after his father had died tragically in a plane crash.

'I remember the crowds, men with swords and flags but I was too young to really understand what was going on. My mother then took me away from here so I could have some normal semblance of growing up, away from the attention, although from time to time I would have to sit with elders and attend functions.'

It struck me that the Maharajah had carried an incredible burden of responsibility since his childhood. The challenge of making his role relevant in modern India, especially after the Constitution removed his princely privileges, was in its own way as big a battle as anything his ancestors had fought.

So? Are the modern maharajahs at all relevant in modern India, the India of the nuclear age and new player at the global poker table? Well, if the Maharajah of Jodhpur and his family are anything to go by, yes, possibly more than ever. It seems to me that in an India in which so much is happening so fast, links with tradition have become ever more important and the royal families provide that sense of continuity. Many of them, despite having been stripped of power and wealth, have not sold up and moved to retirement homes in Goa, but, as Bapji said, they have adapted and perhaps more importantly, they don't intend to go anywhere.

The Eton of India

Another respected Rajasthani institution, Mayo College, has also adapted to serve India in the twenty-first century. Mayo sits in the town of Ajmer about 150 miles east of Jodhpur and is known as the Eton of India. Founded in 1870 at the height of British rule with the aim of giving young Indian Princes a proper public-school education, the school is still highly sought after for the children of modern India's

movers and shakers – politicians, movie producers, industrialists and, of course, maharajahs. The Principal of the school, Mr Pramod Sharma, also just happens to be married to my cousin, Madhuli.

The couple came to visit me at my college when I was in the final year of my degree back in the late 1980s. I was renting a rather cramped attic room at the time, which consisted of two wicker chairs and a double bed. The mattress on the double bed had a sagging crease in it that drew anyone either lying or sitting on it inexorably down into the fold. Being at the top of the house, I had to carefully plan cups of coffee or tea, as it was a long return trip to get a forgotten teaspoon. In addition, one had to make for the lavatory at first skirmish; once hostilities broke out it was way too late to start seeking a ceasefire. I tell you all this, because it was into this environment that my cousin and her relatively new husband at the time came to visit. My parents had told me he was an academic, but as I met him for the first time I was charmed by his good humour, interesting and interested demeanour, and good grace. Neither he nor Madhuli ever mentioned the quicksand aspect of the bed, or that the Jaffa cakes and almond fingers had slowly vanished into the crevasse (I had no table to put them on). Now almost twenty years later, carrying a slight embarrassment of my own previous efforts, I would be taking advantage of their hospitality.

As the crew and I drive through the gates we are faced with the oldest and most impressive building in Mayo, containing the assembly hall and administrative offices. The architecture is at once both austere and decoratively imposing. It's like a cross between a palace and a place of worship, with its turrets, ornate balustrades, pillars and arches, and a tall clock tower topped with the distinctive Queen Victoria crown, emphasizing that nothing or no one was above the crown.

Though the Principal and I have met a couple of times over the years, we have never met in professional circumstances, so when I catch sight of him, I'm not sure whether to hug him or stick with the formal handshake. We end up doing half of each: an informal handshake and

one-armed hug. Principal Sharma ushers me into the assembly hall and I'm accorded a seat on the stage along with the rest of the staff. Glancing round at the besuited gentlemen and soberly dressed ladies around me I suddenly feel a little underdressed. No jacket, no tie. I feel like the PE teacher.

The assembly hall carries large portraits of all of the past Principals and is lined with uncomfortable-looking wooden benches. The boys file in silently and efficiently and take their seats.

The assembly is brief and ends with a secular prayer, as the school embraces multiculturalism despite the pupils being overwhelmingly Hindu. I ask the Principal about this over a post-assembly cup of tea.

Principal Sharma explains: 'In fact Hinduism is secular; the freedom to follow one's beliefs. There are no rules in Hinduism, just a set of guidelines. We try to follow that ethos within the school.'

'But there are rules within the school,' I counter.

'Yes, young minds need boundaries, so discipline is very important. Within that structure, however, the students are encouraged to express themselves.'

Mayo's reputation is such that even Indian parents living in Britain are sending their sons here. I met up with a thirteen-year-old from Enfield, north London and an eleven-year-old from Doncaster to get their impression of the school and see how it compared to the English equivalent.

'We have to get up at 5 a.m. and we do half an hour of physical exercise like karate or gymnastics, then we change and have breakfast and then our lessons start.'

I feel a slight nausea as they say this. Through my childhood I only woke up at 5 a.m. if I'd had a nightmare, apart from two weekends in my teens when I helped deliver milk. The first weekend was when I realized I was doing the longest milk round in western Europe and the second weekend was when I quit.

Both boys had been at Mayo for just over six months and both said it took them a month to stop being homesick and missing things such as English fast food and (slightly bizarrely) the weather – often it just gets too hot for boys used to the breezy temperatures of Blighty. They have one phone call a week home and an email or letter and only see their families during the holidays. Although as a child I thought boarding school an exciting idea, shaped no doubt by the jolly japes in Enid Blyton books (and reinforced as an adult through the *Harry Potter* series), the thought of seeing my own son four times a year and only having one chat a week fills me with unease. I'm beginning to feel nauseous again.

BELOW: The impressive Mayo College. Future captains of Indian industry? The really smart ones ask me for an autograph.

I ask the boys about other differences between Mayo and their former schools.

'There's much more to do here, especially sports and things like debating clubs, music and sculpting. Also sometimes in England if the kids were mucking about, the lesson would stop and we wouldn't learn anything and sometimes the teacher would get fed up and stop.'

'What happens if you muck about here?'

'You have to do half an hour of sit-ups outside.'

I ask the Principal whether the discipline regime is a little harsh on boys so young.

'My approach has always been that the boys must follow their passion and we give them every opportunity to discover that passion by having the widest range of extra-curricular activities possible. Whatever they're interested in, we will try and furnish it for them. Young minds are apt to wander, and if not guided can lead them towards mindless pursuits such as alcohol and drugs. Every young person wants to experiment, so we fill their days with choices, to experiment with different sports or knowledge-based activities; we don't give their minds time to wander.'

The purpose of Mayo when it was launched almost 150 years ago may have been to give India's privileged few a taste of British education, but today its purpose seems to be to turn out confident, independent, well-rounded young men who will become India's ambassadors in the new world order.

As I wander through the school, I find three young boys playing blues rock on electric guitars in the music school and see some quite stunning sketches and designed clothes in the art school. Another group, part of the 'Film Society', stop to ask me for advice on a 30-minute film they've just written, directed and performed in. I think back to my secondary school and recall the extra-curricular activities that were available to me. Well … there was hanging round the tuck shop, hanging round the bike sheds and hanging round just outside the school gates. A music teacher banned me from the piano room, because I didn't have a piano at home – that's why I was playing the one at school … duh! And unless you were in one of the school's sports teams, you didn't get a look in at the sports hall. So my extra-curricular pursuits really amounted to lots of hanging around in various venues, trying to think of something funny to say.

I'm told that some students are playing polo, so I head down to the polo fields where I find a small group of sixth formers watching the match. As young men who are in their final terms at Mayo, imminently to be catapulted into the real world, I wondered what kind of values they were leaving the school with and what their perceptions of modern India were.

'What do you think are the main problems India is facing in the twenty-first century, sixty years after Independence?' I asked, and several of them piped up.

'Poverty is one of the biggest problems but also corruption, you know bribery, especially in politics … child labour, pollution and, of course, population and infrastructure.'

I ask what they think the solutions are.

'Definitely education, especially of the rural masses. Most of India is village based and we have to see to their problems.'

'But,' I say, 'most Indians wouldn't get an education like yours.'

'No, that's true but many poor don't get any kind of education. We should give them basic lessons at least.'

They tell me that India must start striving towards progress, peace and prosperity. It seems they've got the political poster campaign sorted already.

'What do you think Mayo College has given you, how has it shaped you?'

'Mayo has given us everything.' The boys chime in unison. 'We feel

OPPOSITE: Deportment, village style.

ABOVE: Rajasthani goat herders.

we've got the best education and we're not daunted by going anywhere in the world. We've had the chance to learn so many things at Mayo that we feel we can face any problem.'

The polite, confident boys of Mayo are anticipating high-flying careers in the corporate world: law, politics, accountancy, journalism and advertising. One young man predicts that forty years down the line the world will see a new India, and they, the Mayo boys, will be the leaders of this new India.

Incidentally, Principal Sharma and cousin Madhuli were perfect hosts; they graciously never brought out any jaffa cakes, and no almond fingers were pointed mockingly in my direction.

Barefoot

Thirty-five degrees in the shade during the day and down to freezing at night. I awoke early the following morning, feeling rather feverish, and had a strong cup of masala tea to kick-start my senses into life.

I'd spent my first few days in Rajasthan in the company of some of its most privileged inhabitants but I was about to head deeper into the region, to see how basic life is for many of its people and how comprehensively they need help. I was leaving an establishment that caters primarily to the wealthy and advantaged, to one that seeks to benefit 'the poorest of the poor who have no alternatives', Barefoot College.

The drive from Ajmer took about an hour, traversing some of Rajasthan's dry desert brush land and we arrive at a large walled encampment of concrete buildings, interspersed with smaller huts with thatched roofs. As I get out of the car, I see children and adults are wandering about in a relaxed manner, which makes this feel less like a college campus and more like a small village on a late Sunday morning.

A group of philanthropists who believed that solutions to rural problems lay within the community itself set up the college in 1972. Initially, they identified young villagers who had been unable to receive or complete any formal education and who as adults had effectively 'dropped out', but today the college's reputation has reached the point where villagers now approach them.

The emphasis here is on practical skills rather than the traditional areas of reading and writing. Some of this college's alumni would be considered practically illiterate in mainstream society. It's a place where communities attempt to find solutions by themselves, through interdependence. One of the college's most popular schemes teaches people how to make and maintain solar powered lights, a boon in areas with limited electricity. They also learn to purify water. Education and empowerment of women and children, health and sanitation and social awareness are all areas that are covered within its pragmatic curriculum.

The college campus extends over 80,000 square feet and includes residences, a library, a teacher training unit and even an open-air theatre. There's a water-testing laboratory, a craft shop and development centre and a 700,000-litre rainwater-harvesting tank. The college is completely solar-electrified and reaches over 125,000 people in both immediate and distant areas.

The central idea is that people learn practical knowledge and skills that they can take back to the villages rather than giving them a paper qualification that they can take to the cities. They embrace one of Mahatma Gandhi's principles that rural India should adopt new technologies, but only if the people could own and maintain it themselves, thus lessening the opportunities for exploitation. I chatted to Vasu, one of the founders of the college.

'One always comes back to the people's basic minimum needs: water, energy, education and livelihood. Once they have that, then they can contribute creatively to the greater society … caste, gender, religion have no place here. People here understand that to gain a better life, everyone has to work together.'

(The caste system is one of the traditional forms of social hierarchy in India. Hardly any mention is made of it in any of the Hindu scriptures, though it evolved into a religious and ultimately political tool, whereby 'Brahmans', the top caste, were accorded most respected status and the untouchables or 'Dalits', as they are known today, were the bottom of the pile. They were given the most menial jobs in society and offered the least assistance. Today, though the importance of caste is diluted in the large urban sprawls, it is still regarded very highly in many rural areas and remains a fertile ground for political and economic exploitation.)

The college also benefits city dwellers too, Vasu tells me.

'Our cities are getting ever-more overcrowded, mainly because of migration from the rural areas. If the quality of life in the villages is improved, we may be able to even reverse that trend. Also we found that many urbanites began to visit Barefoot College where they gained a sense of perspective, by having to focus on the things that are really important, rather than worrying about how many TV sets you have, or getting the latest household gadget. In fact, many of these city dwellers have returned to help spread the message or have become supporters of the college.'

At lunch I got talking to Mungibai, a middle-aged woman and

former student of Barefoot College. She belongs to a low-caste background and is now the education coordinator at the college. She faced opposition from her husband and the menfolk in her village for even attending the college, but she tells me that they've got used to it now and have supported the empowerment of other women from her village.

As there is no differentiation between castes and genders, she tells me that even in the dining area, each individual is responsible for picking up and rinsing their plates. She indicates the hand pump in the courtyard and then gives me a Paddington Bear hard stare. I get the message.

One of Mungibai's current responsibilities is coordinating Barefoot College's 'children's parliament'. The parliament provides a regular forum where children who attend the dozens of night schools sponsored by the college can get together to discuss their education needs and report back on how well they think they've been taught. None of these children is able to attend a regular day school, as they are out working their family land.

The children are encouraged to go through the democratic process of electing a Prime Minister and other important posts, to understand early on why getting involved in the process of representation is important. The ministerial posts (including a 'Minister of Play') are rotated regularly and all issues relating to children are debated in an open forum.

'Our main challenge,' says Vasu, 'is reaching the educated person who ignorantly believes that rural villagers are dimwits who don't know anything. Ironically, in India the educated are themselves acting as a barrier to education for the poor.'

As I watch the calm goings on of Barefoot College, I begin to feel dizzy. Though the sun is doing its job by blazing overhead, I am shivering. I then get a nosebleed that's so severe, I look like the last ten minutes of a Tarantino movie.

I fear my Rajasthani curse has struck me again.

BELOW: Chatting with Vasu at Barefoot College. By this time I had a fever of 104, but couldn't fail to be impressed with the project.

CHAPTER TWELVE

A Camel Called Sanjeev

By the time I'd reached the hotel I was having an out of body experience. The shivering was uncontrollable, and it was possibly the worst time to be asked for an autograph, but I managed a drunken scrawl, retired to my room and called a doctor. He informed me that I was running a fever of 104 degrees and a pulse that was racing. I also had a chesty cough that refused to abate.

The doctor, a middle-aged man, had recently returned to India with his family after living in Britain for more than twenty years. He had been a GP in Leicester but had returned to India to open his own clinic and now had full administrative control as well as support staff. He suggested I have a blood test. Part of India's climb up the golden ladder of prosperity has been due to the huge labour force, and even taking blood becomes a labour-intensive operation.

Three people arrived to take my blood – the actual guy (who looked about 12 years old) and his two assistants. One handed things like the syringe and the vial to the blood guy, and the other … I'm not absolutely certain what his function was. He seemed to be there for comic relief, as he wandered about bumping into things and falling over. I'm not totally convinced he was there for my benefit.

OPPOSITE: Jain Holy Hill and Temple complex, Mount Girnar, Junagadh, Gujarat.

The doctor informed me I'd picked up fairly common virus in these parts for this time of year and sent through the items on the prescription, including a linctus containing Codeine. This was very effective but when I checked the label on the bottle I was slightly taken aback. There were the contents and instructions as per normal, but also, in a little yellow star, in the middle of the label were the words 'New Tingle Flavour!' I'm not sure what flavour 'tingle' is or where it comes from, but it struck me that the prescription medicine market in India must be pretty damn competitive if 'New Tingle Flavour' becomes the unique selling proposition that gives you the edge over your rivals.

After a week of catarrh, coughs and capsules I was ready to get back out there and complete my Rajasthani sojourn.

Camel light

It's perhaps all too easy to forget that India's high-tech cities simply can't carry this enormous nation into the new millennium on their own; the vast majority of India's billion-plus population live in rural areas and it's out here that progress is most desperately needed. I'd seen the kind of efforts that were being made to help these real 'village people' through the work at Barefoot College and the Maharajah of Jodhpur's projects. But I'd also heard that amongst the most precarious communities in Rajasthan were the nomadic camel herders, so I decided to venture into the desert.

Hanwant Singh Rathore works for the LPPS, a welfare organization for livestock keepers, set up in 1996 to support 'Raika' camel pastoralists in acute crisis in Rajasthan. He's promised me an introduction to some of the few remaining camel herders but warns me that, 'Herders have been in this region for centuries, and there's one group that has about a hundred and twenty camels in the area – but being nomads, it may take some time to find them.'

This is the dry brush part of the desert, as opposed to the undulating 'Lawrence of Arabia'-style sand dunes which one can find about sixty miles west of here. We drive along dirt tracks and off road, with Hanwant guiding us through sparse vegetation – arid-looking trees with spikey leaves – and along routes that the Raika camel herders have taken in the past. A phone call prompts Hanwant to call a halt to our two-car convoy. Apparently the camels are coming. Eventually, a cloud of dust in the distance grows and envelops us.

I've never seen such a large congregation of long spindly legs. As they get closer I ask Hanwant if there are any ground rules for dealing with camels: don't look them in the eye, don't touch their knees without being asked, don't swear … that kind of thing.

'No, no rules, these camels are entirely domesticated, reared for milk, not at all dangerous.'

As the gaggle of cheerful creatures saunters past me, I find it easy to believe him.

They stop occasionally for a snack of thorny leaves. 'Camels don't eat any vegetation from the ground,' Hanwant tells me; 'only from the branches of the tall trees.'

These animals seem a lot taller in the flesh than they do on TV. The Indian camel, I'm told, is the tallest of all, African camels being considerably smaller.

One of the herders, a wizened elderly man (actually they're all old and, indeed, a bit wizened) approaches me and proffers a small metal bowl. 'Camel milk,' he says in the local dialect.

Having only just recovered from my virus with the aid of 'New Tingle Flavour', I was in no way going to jeopardize my health by ingesting camel product. But on the other hand, when was I ever going to do this again? I took a sip and then a moment to see if I could sense any message my bowels were trying to convey to me.

'Actually, this isn't bad!' I told the herder.

The milk didn't taste too different from regular cow's milk, perhaps a little saltier. Then a rather obvious thought struck me.

'Has this just come out of the camel?' I asked, trying to turn my grimace into a smile.

'Yes,' the herder grinned.

'What, just now?' I asked a little more accusingly than I had intended.

'Oh yes,' replied the herder.

Well that explains why it was a little warm. I feel momentarily queasy, but it's the thought of the milk's recent journey rather than the actual taste. The moment passes without any internal messages.

Grazing time was over and we joined the herders as they headed back to their camp for the night. The camp was basically just an open space rather than any constructed site. At the camp I met Dr Ilse Kohler-Rollefson, a German vet who's worked extensively in the Middle East and North Africa, but chose to stay in Rajasthan because of the desperate plight of the herders. I ask her why, after generations of nomadic life, there should be particular difficulty now.

'Today they literally have no place to graze their camels anymore. Most of the camels are not in terribly good condition. Their humps are small; they wander the fields but are rarely rewarded with much to eat anymore. If the number of miscarriages within the herd continues, they may be forced to give up their livelihood.'

'How can the camel herders survive?' I ask.

'It's been difficult,' Ilse tells me. 'The younger generation don't want to do this anymore and have moved to the cities. That's hard for the herders to take because some of these families have been herding for many generations and feel it's their divine duty to herd. So we're looking into developing new camel-related products. Their most lucrative resource is camel milk, which contains many fantastic health qualities such as being low in cholesterol which is particularly good for people suffering from diabetes, and from the milk also camel ice cream.'

'Camel flavoured?' I ask.

'Caramel,' Ilse corrects me.

'Hey, you could call the range Camel Light!' I tell her.

Ilse smiles politely, giving my comment the non-reaction it deserves. She asks me if I have ever been kissed by a camel. I laugh before I realize she's actually waiting for an answer.

'No, but come close many times … really? Kissed by a camel?'

'It's lovely,' the tall German doctor tells me with a twinkle in her eye. 'You should try it … let's find one for you.'

'Now?' I splutter.

She finally finds her favourite camel. 'This is Meera.'

'That's my wife's name!' I laugh.

ABOVE: The Pushkar Camel Fair is where most herders go when selling up. Piercing the camels' noses is traditional after a sale.

Seeing as there's really not enough time for me and the camel to get properly acquainted (it would have to be a movie and dinner at least!), I allow 'Meera' to give me the camel equivalent of a peck on the cheek. More of a brushing of the lips, than anything more sordid, I'm happy to report.

Over some tea, with camel milk of course, I sit down beside the fire with Ilse, Hanwant and the herders. The elderly herders chat quietly and chew small amounts of opium. They seem a little reserved but there's also an air of sad resignation about them. Dusk is beginning to descend and I can't help feeling a tinge of sadness for them, watching a scene that wouldn't have changed for centuries. Ilse tells me that if this year turns out to be a lean one, they might sell their entire herd at the Rajasthan camel fair held in the autumn.

As I'm saying my final thank yous and goodbyes, there's a sudden burst of activity. Nearby, a pregnant camel has started to give birth and the calf's head and legs have emerged. A herder starts tugging frantically on the calf's exposed quarters, and within minutes it's all over. The mother looks entirely unfazed, as if this sort of thing happens to her all the time.

I feel rather emotional at the whole thing, perhaps because of becoming a father recently myself, and I find myself silently and desperately willing the new calf to pull through and survive. The relative silence makes it all a little eerie, but after about ten minutes, the newborn is out. Ilse ushers us away to allow mother and baby time to bond. But as the frail little creature lies wet and still on the dusty ground it's hard to tell what fate has in store for it. The calf then waves its scrawny camel neck about and everyone breathes a sigh of relief. The baby is alive and the important bonding process begins, the mother sniffing and nudging her offspring with her snout as the baby nuzzles at her head.

'Isn't that wonderful?' Ilse whispers, her passion for her work undiminished even after all these years.

It turns out that the new addition to the herd is a boy; Ingrid tells me they will call it Sanjeev.

House of the great soul

It's time for me to re-engage with the atmosphere of urban India the following morning, as I get off the plane in Ahmedabad, Gujarat – it's like stepping into a completely different country. This city was once known as the Manchester of the East because of its thriving industry: textiles, pharmaceuticals and light industry. It's perhaps even better known as the place where Mahatma Gandhi started his ashram community in 1915 and launched his campaign for Indian independence.

I have very mixed feelings about visiting Gujarat. At first glance, it's celebrated as the birthplace of Mahatma Gandhi, whose message of non-violence and peaceful coexistence made him one of the most important figures in global history.

Yet this state also saw some of the worst communal violence that India has experienced in recent years. In 2002, around a thousand

ABOVE: Gandhiji's humble abode at his ashram. People were being butchered just a few hundred yards from this place. Shame, shame, shame.

people, 75 per cent of whom were Muslim, were murdered in riots targeting the community by right-wing Hindu mobs. This was in supposed retaliation for 58 Hindu pilgrims burned to death in a train. The ensuing tit-for-tat violence lasted almost 10 weeks. The repercussions of Independence are still being felt, it seems. Gandhi, the founding father of an undivided and unified India, and devotee of non-violent protest, would have been truly appalled.

The first place I visit in Ahmedabad is his famous ashram, where Gandhi developed key aspects of his philosophy and had countless meetings with other players in India's Independence movement as well as foreign journalists. The ashram is calm and well maintained, the buzz of traffic from the main road a distant hum. Tourists and devotees alike take photographs, and students from local colleges sit on the grassy areas, engrossed in their textbooks.

I wander through the small museum depicting Gandhiji, as he's known respectfully in India. There are a few letters, a few photographs and many of his quotes on display. I stop and take in a few:

'The Seven Deadly Sins are wealth without work, pleasure without conscience, knowledge without character, business without morality, science without humanity, worship without sacrifice and politics without principle.'

'There are people in the world so hungry, that God cannot appear to them except in the form of bread.'

'I am prepared to die, but there is no cause for which I am prepared to kill.'

I'm reminded by these of how wise and unique he was. He inspired a nation to confront an empire through peaceful protest, and as I walk past the various exhibits I think of how senseless his assassination was – shot dead by a right-wing Hindu just six months after Indian Independence.

Gandhiji's home is also preserved here, a simple four-room bungalow and, as a special treat, I've been allowed into the Mahatma's private room, not normally open to the public. A bamboo mat and two cushions make up Gandhi's seat.

Here he would sit and receive leaders from around the world. The only other furniture in the room are two small chairs for visitors, one complete with a tiny statue of the three monkeys representing speak no evil, see no evil, hear no evil, and of course the symbolic spinning wheel, as to Gandhi home-spun cloth represented self-sufficiency.

Though I have a slightly rebellious urge to sit on his mat, I can't bring myself to do it. I have too much respect for the man and his legacy and I'm honoured to have been given access his private space. Given all the unrest and conflict across our planet today, I wonder where today's Gandhi is? What leader or statesman carries his legacy?

The room reflects the simple standard of living Gandhi promoted, and his simple, clear message of tolerance and non-violence. It seems a real shame that as a practising Hindu he would sit in this room and receive anyone who wished to see him, and that in this part of India only a few years ago this message was so completely forgotten. His peaceful bequest lost, along with the lives of countless men, women and children.

On a lighter note, it suddenly strikes me how ironic it is, given Gandhiji's message to 'Only possess that what you need', that his image appears on the Indian currency, the Rupee.

To try to get an unbiased portrait of what happened in Gujarat is not easy, but sitting on a bench at the ashram, overlooking the river,

I spoke with a local Jesuit priest, Father Cedric Prakash. He saw people being butchered on the streets, houses ablaze. The violence came as a huge shock to him, that man could be so inhuman to man.

I ask if there was any explanation for the degree to which it went, in this Mahatma Gandhi's state.

'It was madness, a blood lust, I was watching people being beaten and stabbed … police in some situations were powerless because of the size of the mobs and times chose simply to do nothing … I did whatever I could to help the injured.'

'Was it just a mass letting loose of anger or was it more orchestrated?' I asked him.

'People were targeting specific homes. In mixed areas, Muslims' houses were pointed out, even by their neighbours, Muslim-owned shops with Hindu names were smashed up.'

This was so reminiscent of the violence of Partition, and I shudder at the thought of all this going on just outside the walls of Gandhiji's ashram.

'But,' I ask, 'if this was about communal tension between Hindus and Muslims, how come the bloodletting didn't extend beyond the borders of Gujarat, or indeed to the whole of Gujarat?'

'Exactly,' answers Father Cedric. 'That suggests that it was not communally but politically motivated. In many parts of the state and in neighbouring states, there was no violence at all. Very sad, very sad.' He shakes his head.

'What about the aftermath? How has it been since?' I ask.

'Many believe those responsible for initiating the violence, the perpetrators of the violence, still roam the streets with impunity and with great immunity. We need to look into the role the government played, the role of the law and order machinery, the fact that many people feel today, even five years down the line, that the victims of the Gujarat carnage have not got their just due.'

Gujarat remains a highly polarized world, and yet Cedric remains hopeful. The fact that there are Indians committed to communal

OPPOSITE: Narmada River, Gujarat. The variety of scenery within any Indian state can leave the viewer breathless – this looks like an oil painting.

OVERLEAF: Away from the industrial cities, Gujarat has incredible sights like this Jain Temple.

harmony, justice and peace should, ultimately, lead to India's prosperity in the years to come.

One of Father Cedric's local initiatives was the instigation of a local cricket team, and he took me to a barren piece of land right next to the scenes of some of the worst violence in 2002. In the early evening light, a match was in full swing. Dodging the odd ball flying past my head, I managed to grab a few words with some of the players. The unusual and heartening point of these matches are that the teams are entirely mixed, comprising young Hindus and Muslims sharing their passion for the sport. In short snatches of conversation and with their eyes following the game avidly, the boys, all in their teens, told me how frightening those awful days were.

RIGHT: Cricket, India's sporting obsession, played literally everywhere.

I ask what sort of reaction the cricketers get from their neighbour-hoods for playing in a mixed team. One young man tells me that feelings are varied, often discouraging as well as encouraging; however, they try to ignore these and concentrate on enjoying the sport.

'Cricket is the way forward,' one lad tells me. 'Who doesn't like cricket? There should be more mixed teams like this; after all, the Indian national team is mixed.'

Finally, I ask them if they have hope for the future.

'What else is there?' One of the smart young boys asks me flatly.

'There's you,' I tell the little group.

Crossing the Channel by bicycle

The following morning I feel the need to be cheered up a bit after yesterday's tales of gratuitous violence. The crew and I drive to the local university's grounds for a science fair with a difference. It's a science fair for new inventors run by the 'Honey Bee Network'. Its founder, a charismatic management professor named Anil Gupta, shows me around the small exhibits.

'Honey Bee Network was set up to access the wealth of innovation that exists in our villages. These grassroots inventors will find ways of making their lives easier that are ingenious, necessarily inexpensive and something that professionals wouldn't have thought of.'

In the early morning light, few people are wandering about the fair, which is a rather grand term for about twenty tables containing varied and downright weird contraptions.

I spy a bicycle connected to a large metal box. Professor Gupta sparks up: 'An exercise bike and also a washing machine. You pedal here and the wheel chain rotates the drum. Simple.'

Other devices are an aid to chop wheat; a food stall that redirects heat from the hot plate into a boiler, thus saving energy in making tea; and, most fascinating to me, cow-dung batteries. Ten little boxes wired together contain old, used batteries nestled in cow dung. I'm genuinely astonished when the villager whose brain child this is connects two little wires to a transistor radio that then obediently blares out Bollywood music, as if it were plugged into the mains.

Professor Gupta excitedly points at the boxes.

'These ten little boxes can produce a current of up to twelve volts for a whole month and have been used to operate lights, charge mobile phones and, as you can see, radios. In fact any electrical appliance can be charged if enough boxes are added, all you do is add a little saline solution to the cow dung which in turn keeps these dead batteries alive and –' he invites me to sniff '– there's no smell.'

This is India's version of Green Energy. I do point out that for the folks back home, the concept of ten boxes of bullshit might be a little hard to sell, but the display is mightily impressive.

For the final demonstration, we have to get back in our cars and travel ten minutes to a small manmade lake. There, an ancient-looking maverick awaits us, aboard what seems to be a Chitty Chitty Bang Bang-style bicycle, complete with tin floats, makeshift propellers and flags.

Professor Gupta is still exuberant: 'This man is in his eighties and has been finessing his water bicycle for many years now … he had the idea after his area was flooded.'

The old guy pedals as fast as he can, the single propeller turning lethargically and the whole aqua experience crawling through the water like a duck with a hangover.

'What applications could this possibly have?' I ask the Professor.

'Well, it could be a water sport,' he says, laughing. 'Removing weeds from lakes, or for vendors selling small baskets of produce.'

They all seem a little desperate to me.

'His dream is to cross the English Channel,' adds Gupta.

Personally, I don't fancy his chances.

The old man's follow-up invention, 'water skating shoes' – two mini papier-mâché canoes strapped to his feet – strike me as even less practical than the bike. The professor tells me that this adventurous old man is an inspiration to young people who see what can still be achieved at his age. The crowds that have inevitably gathered cheer the pensioner on enthusiastically.

As our crew film him, and teenagers peer down at his creations from above the lake, the Professor tells me that after a hard life this man has now finally had his day in the sun, simply by us filming him. As he steps back ashore he gives me a hug, sheds a few tears and says he was given a promise that one day he would conquer the world, and today he feels like he's done just that.

It feels good to leave Ahmedabad on a more inspired note after hearing so much about the shameless violence of recent times. Tomorrow morning I'm heading south, to Pune, and to an idealized vision of India's future.

City of tomorrow

'Life as it should be. Imagine a day when you get up early after a good night's sleep, look out of your window and see greenery everywhere. Absolute calm prevails. You don your walking shoes and greet your neighbours, who are more like good friends, the sunrays darting through the trees into your tranquillity. You then smell that fresh pure oxygenated air. God, it feels good.'

BELOW: Magarpatta City. A vision of the future?

So reads the advertising blurb for a place called Magarpatta City on the outskirts of Pune. It's basically an integrated, gated community, which has been designed for the high-achieving networked society of the new millennium.

The flight from Ahmedabad is mercifully short. As I approach the final city in my trek around India, the complimentary nuts and in-flight savoury snacks have lost their novelty and allure.

Pune is a large town referred to, by some, as the 'Detroit of India' due to its history of automotive industries. It sits high on a plateau about 75 miles east of Bombay and is as lush and green as Bangalore. In fact it has seen an explosion of IT-related industries similar to Bangalore and has also embraced mall culture, with wine bars, designer shops and multiplexes.

The walled commune is about four miles from the centre of Pune and we pass through into the city after a brief but thorough security check at the main gate. The main gate gives the impression of a theme park or movie studio more than a primarily residential area, with the name 'Magarpatta City' writ large over the gateway entrance. Almost forty thousand residents leave and enter the city through these gates.

The roads within are broad and spotless with traffic being almost non-existent. There's a homogeneity to the various enclaves within the city, all of them clean, white buildings with solar panels on the roofs and carefully maintained fauna and flora.

I approach a block of apartments and the sign outside informs me these flats are called 'Erica', and underneath is the statement, 'A life of eternal bliss'. I'm visiting a family living in one of these peaceful abodes, to find out whether living here is truly 'eternal bliss'.

The couple and their young daughter don't have a very large or luxurious house, but they have what they think everyone should be entitled to: 'quality of life, a peaceful one, with easy access parking'.

'We used to spend hours travelling every day; dropping our daughter to school and then travelling through Pune's terrible traffic to

work. Now everything is walking distance, we have more of the day to actually be a family.'

With schools, shops, sports facilities and offices within the walls of the city, there seems to be little reason to travel outside. Part of the city's appeal is that there everything anyone would need is a walk away, including restaurants and large open verdant spaces. There's talk of a multiplex, theatre and even a university being built here too.

'What would you say to those who might term this place as elitist?' I ask the couple.

'Yes,' they answer, 'it is, though we're not cut off from the outside world; we still meet people from outside.'

Curious. The mini-city is a self-contained bubble that shields privileged eyes from the realities of the dirty streets outside. Outside the apartment block, teenagers and children play basketball and gather to meet their friends. The streets are cleaned as security guards look on.

Magarpatta was the brainchild of Mr Satish Magar, the Chairman and Managing Director of Magarpatta Township Development & Construction Company Limited.

He's so successful (and proud) that he now has a city named after him. I meet with him at a central multi-cuisine café, across the road from Cybercity Magarpatta, the glass-fronted IT offices at the heart of the complex. Almost twenty companies have offices here, providing jobs for many of Magarpatta's residents.

I ask him whether there is an optimum size to a development like Magarpatta, before they become so big that they are in danger of experiencing the same municipal and civic problems as the world outside?

'I would say the threshold is anything between six to seven thousand residential units and four to five million square feet of space [the size of Magarpatta], as beyond this the city would become unmanageable.'

I later discover that the Indian government has now restricted the size of new developments to 200 acres, one third of the size of Magarpatta. Over the next few decades India will see a lot of these manufactured worlds popping up all over the country – Mr Magar is set to build three more in the Pune area alone.

Although there aren't special conditions to buying a residency here, it is clearly aimed at the increasing middle classes. One needs to organize a mortgage to live here and that pretty much leaves out all those on low incomes … the majority of Indians in fact.

There's definitely a campus feel to the city. With so much open space and its own police force, parents do not have the same worries as those outside Magarpatta – if their child is lost they are lost within the safe confines of the city gates. One of things that impress me about the city is its emphasis on being eco-friendly. Residents have their own water-harvesting facilities, and solar power (utilizing a resource that India has plenty of) is used to heat water and therefore bring down living costs. Recycled garbage is being used for bio-fuel, which again helps save money.

As a result of the success of Magarpatta, I ask whether Mr Magar thinks there is a danger that these developments could draw the middle classes away from the traditional city centres and leave them as slightly dead zones.

'I don't think so,' he says. 'There will always be migration to the cities and also there are people who prefer to live in city centres rather than suburbs.'

There aren't any cows in here, or for that matter any non-domestic animals. Mr Magar points out that if there were, the lush greenery of the city's communal spaces and residential gardens would not last long. 'If we found a cow in here, we would eject them … in the nicest possible way.'

Finally I say to him, 'It is possible in twenty years or so, to have a situation whereby a child has been born here, schooled here and works here – they won't have to deal with poverty, beggars, or even rubbish on the streets. Will that prepare them for dealing with the real world outside Magarpatta's walls?'

'That's true,' he answers, surprisingly honestly, 'it's a possibility. That

will be a challenge for children grown up here and something we may have to consider.'

Although there's no doubt that Magarpatta is a very impressive environment, especially for a family with security and conservation high on their personal list, I don't see any sign of rebellious creativity. It's refreshing to see such a high degree of civic responsibility – no graffiti, no random trash in the streets, or indeed traffic volume – but equally at this early stage, no individual flair. No one has stuck a joyously ludicrous statue in their front garden or painted their house blue or covered their property in bunting. I guess right now, people are enjoying the novelty of the regularity of the city but I can't wait to see it in about ten years time. The big question being: will the cows have found a way in?

ABOVE: One of the three in this picture wouldn't be allowed in Magarpatta City.

Silver surfers

The following morning, my last day in Pune, I'm joining a special gathering at an apartment in the city centre. I have seen modern India adapting to meet the needs of becoming a global player in all sorts of ways, through commerce, rural initiatives, in a spiritual sense and through entertainment, and today I'm seeing an organization that aims to help a very specific group of older citizens.

NRIPO (Non Resident Indians' Parents' Organization) has been set up by families to help Indian parents whose children are all abroad. This is much more than a social club. Without their kids to turn to, this group of elderly residents has formed their own alternative family to rely on.

Non Resident Indians (NRIs) have become a force to be reckoned with around the world. Today the Indian diaspora is second only to that of China, and a huge number of middle-class Indian families has a son or daughter working or studying in the US, Canada, Australia or Europe. While it's brought money, prestige and cultural diversity to the family left behind, this emigration has also left a gaping hole at the centre of family life, and NRIPO is there to plug that gap.

Traditional Indian culture places an enormous amount of emphasis on the family, especially as a support system. Living as an extended family is still the norm and as the parents get older, responsibility is passed on to the younger members of the family.

Although the idea of grandparents, parents, their kids and even a daughter- or son-in-law sharing the same living space may fill you, dear reader, with a cold clammy fear, it does provide a wonderful sense of community and continuity to the youngest members of the family. Over the last twenty years there has been a move away from these huge homesteads, as kids have moved away, but still for the majority of the older generation, the extended family is an appealing state.

The parents I'm meeting this morning remind me of the gaggle of aunts and uncles I would encounter whenever I visited India as a child.

LEFT: The family waited and waited but still Ramesh could not think of a charade on his wedding day.

Everyone talks at once, tea and biscuits punctuate stories and anecdotes and there is much gentle mockery of one another. Today, I feel like I am a surrogate son to all twenty-two people in the room. The atmosphere is warm and enveloping. Thankfully my face remains un-tweaked.

At first their organization was started as a sort of crisis response group, one member tells me:

'My children are in America and in the middle of the night my husband suffered a heart attack. NRIPO members were at my side

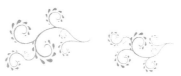

immediately and when he died they helped with funeral arrangements. My children were so far, that they couldn't get back quickly. I don't know what I would have done without them.'

I ask them whether it was a difficult decision to send their children abroad, or even to allow them to go? Many of them left to get degrees and then chose not come back.

This was obviously a difficult experience for these parents, fraught with conflicting emotions – on the one hand being proud their children are doing so well, and on the other devastated at them being so far away. One parent says, tongue firmly planted in cheek, 'I'm glad my kids are away. If they hadn't gone I wouldn't have had the chance to have all these foreign holidays whenever I visit them.'

Another pipes in: 'Also we wouldn't have had the opportunities to take part in all the activities.'

'Activities?' I ask.

'Yes, NRIPO isn't just for the difficult times. We have get-togethers, picnics, dramas, music and dancing. Every member takes part in the dramas, giving us a chance to try something new, challenging and exciting.'

A dapper man wearing a hat at a rakish angle adds: 'I'm a pretty good actor now and I found out through the dramas we put on here; you better watch out!'

The group explode into peals of laughter.

With their children on the other side of the world, these Pune residents have found the emotional support they need, and that sense of community, from each other. They have a scheme whereby one family is taken care of by two other families, so that in the event of one family going to visit their children abroad, the other will be available for support, a touching idea that means no one will ever be left on their own.

They all have web cams, and they talk animatedly about how being able to see their children and talk freely helps them feel more involved in their lives.

'The best thing about the web cams is that for those of us who are grandparents, we can see our grandchildren and they can see us, we are part of each others' lives even though we're thousands and thousands of miles apart.'

'Before NRIPO I didn't even know how to use the video recorder, but now I'm a computer expert,' says one chap.

'But you still don't know how to work the video recorder!' his wife adds quickly. Once again, amid much jovial finger pointing, the group crack up laughing.

This is truly extraordinary. Men and women who grew up without computers have become techno-geeks so that they can stay in touch with the grandchildren.

I ask whether they had ever been tempted to move abroad to be with their children. The concept of moving to the US, UK or Australia does not cause the same animated discussion as my previous questions. All of them have green cards but certainly wouldn't leave India for good.

'This is home,' a lady tells me. 'Why would we want to leave home and this new family?'

'India is cool now,' adds the man with the dapper hat.

The get together is brought to a close by the arrival of lunch, but before we all tuck in, I'm presented with a little wooden award.

'All our children, when they visit, have a big party thrown by us and get this little token to take back with them, to remember us. We hope you remember us too.'

These 'tokens' are then handed out to each of our crew members on this trip. I feel really moved by the unconditional affection and generosity meted out by this group of virtual strangers.

Having traversed much of India on my travels, this group of elderly residents here in Pune go a long way to define my journey. These people are adapting to a new India, but they're doing it with warmth, hope and with each other.

For me, it's time to leave Pune for Mumbai and home to London.

EPILOGUE

Turn On, Tune In, Drop Out

Mumbai/Bombay is exactly how I left it. Humid, buzzing, chaotic, wonderful.

On my last afternoon, I take a cab ride down to the Gateway of India, the large, ornate concrete arch built to commemorate the arrival of King George V in 1911. It was also the place from where the last British troops left India in February 1948. This afternoon, it is humming with tourists and locals, waiting to catch the many ferries that depart from this point. It is perhaps a good place to reflect.

As the sun readies itself for its final trajectory towards the Arabian Sea, I watch a limousine pull in to the 5-star hotel behind the Gateway. A beggar and a couple of hawkers turn away nonchalantly and turn their attentions to the next business opportunity. They make momentary eye contact with me before turning away. I must be blending in!

India remains a dizzying edifice of extremes. Goddesses are worshipped and women have occupied the most powerful positions in the land, and yet it is a male-dominated society. It is the largest democracy in the world and yet a significant proportion of the population are illiterate. The wealth divide between the 'haves' and the 'have nots' is increasing dramatically as India becomes a global player. The destitute

BELOW: The Brits woz here! The Gateway of India in southern Mumbai.

281

number almost 500 million – and that's a hell of a lot of 'have nots'. If the gulf becomes unbridgeable, then what will happen to this underclass? Revolution has traditionally come from this group of people and half a billion voices can make a heck of a noise.

Since Independence, although successive governments have struggled to support this vast underclass, India has made remarkable progress. It has become self-sufficient in basic foodstuff provision, it has a space-exploration programme, it has joined the nuclear club and, after embracing limited free market economics in the early 1990s, has become one of the world's fastest growing economies. And as I saw at Bangalore, India is one of the planet's leading centres for software solutions.

Staring along the waterfront I see many of the 'lower class' folk – hawkers and peddlers and the like – and wonder whether they're aware or even care about 'shining India'. But I do notice a possible trickle-down effect of mass technological advancement. They all have mobile phones: rickshaw wallahs, tuk tuk drivers, the guy selling novelty trumpets – all those people that in India are regarded as the poor working class. Is there a brand new breed of super underclass rising in India? Those 'have nots' without even a mobile phone?

This suggests much more to me than merely some poor people can now phone each other and talk about how poor they are. The growing sophistication of cell phones means that vast numbers of what were regarded as the uneducated and impoverished have access to information via the internet and, more importantly, political groups have a way of accessing them. That could make them a very powerful lobby group indeed.

To the novice traveller, the huge social divide between the pitiably poor and the obscenely wealthy can feel unjust and jarring. However the poor don't spend all their time wondering how they can break into the homes of their rich neighbours and steal all their stuff. Hinduism is fundamentally a fatalistic philosophy; if you were born rich or born poor, it was meant to be. Just be the best person you can and perhaps in the next life you will reap the benefits. It's this attitude that I feel

sapped the ambition of the country to do better in years gone by, but Indians are waking up to the fact that being ambitious and fatalistic are not mutually exclusive. The resultant 'new' India is therefore materially aspirational and yet has a solid moral centre. In a recent poll conducted amongst the kind of young middle-class employees I met at Infosys, over 80 per cent of these modern whiz-kids stated that having a faith was important.

Despite the rapid influx of western influences via the internet, television and high street fashions, India retains a highly traditional core. The celebrations I witnessed – Diwali and the Kali *puja* in Calcutta, the Aarti in Varanasi and, especially, the wonderful Holi in Rishikesh – have not fundamentally changed for hundreds of years. This is in stark contrast to the West where Christmas has moved from midnight mass to mass marketing and Easter has been infiltrated by bunnies and chocolate (both of which receive scant reference in the New Testament).

The high regard for tradition in India also constantly reconfirms the family as the nucleus of society. Young credit-happy urbanites still look to the family as their main reference for self-definition.

ABOVE: The beauty of India's heritage. Gadi Sagar Temple and Lake, Jaisalmer, Rajasthan – a large sandstone gate is said to have been erected here, at the entrance to this stunning, medievel reservoir by a prostitute just to offend the local King. Can't really see the street walkers of London doing that!

283

The fact that 'family' in India means 'extended family' is that a sense of community is still seen as vital. From the camel herders to the elite of Magarpatta City, all seek a sense of community. This, in turn, is what I believe fuels the famed 'Indian hospitality'. The greatest and most humble honour that can be bestowed on a stranger is to be invited into someone's home and be regarded as family.

The crowds at the Gateway chatter noisily as two ferries arrive simultaneously, each circling the other like bloated wrestlers, vying for the 'mooring first' prize. Hindus, Muslims, two Sikhs and a nun move forward, tickets held aloft like Mao's little red book.

I remain impressed with India's steadfast commitment to secularism. Enshrined in the constitution is the freedom to follow your faith. Despite occasional, horrific examples of sectarian violence, most notably the anti-Sikh riots in 1984 and the Hindu-Muslim riots in Gujarat in 2002, India's sizeable religious minorities have continued to co-exist peacefully with the majority Hindus. I was constantly heartened by the various attempts to keep secularism in the picture. The joint worship at the Hindu-Buddhist temple in Darjeeling, Mayo College's secular education, the inclusive ideals at Barefoot College and even the modern egalitarianism of Infosys in Bangalore all point towards an attitude that is under threat in the world's current obsession with religious differences and from zealous Hindu groups within India.

Against the glorious backdrop of the Himalayas, Mark Tully had talked of India's incredible ability to absorb different cultures and yet remain resolutely Indian. It is remarkable that the largest democracy on the planet can happily absorb seemingly contradictory positions: Marxist states such as Kerala and capitalist dynamos such as Bangalore and Mumbai. That Barefoot College serving the needy and Mayo college serving the needless exist just a few miles from each other. A country that is still essentially socialist which embraces and perhaps even needs its royal families.

India somehow functions, even flourishes, consigning all attempts to understand why to the analytical dustbin. India is an experience, not

OPPOSITE: Who ordered the deep pan Margherita? Dancing at one of the many Hindu festivals is an intrinsic part of celebrating the joy of life.

an argument. The whole of humanity is played out in front of your eyes. Everything from birth to death and all points in between, assaults your senses all the time. You can't look away hoping to avoid humanity because you'll simply see that it has moved, changed shape and is challenging you once again from a different angle. Life – India – in all its wonderful and terrible guises, dares you to accept it all.

If you give yourself up to India, she will give herself up to you.

I step away from the commotion at the Gateway and hail a cab to the airport. As we wend our way through the perennial Mumbai traffic marmalade, I realize more fully how many of the signs and billboards are in English.

Britain has, of course, left an indelible mark on India. The railways and the civil service come to mind. As someone once said to me many years ago, 'Britain gave India bureaucracy and India perfected it'. The English language is spoken by over 250 million people and is still the commercial lingua franca of India. Despite the influx of American pop culture, Britain is still held in high regard, seen as the country of high moral values, impeccable manners and of tolerance and taste; the land of Shakespeare, Dickens, Keats and the Beatles … but only just. Media access is allowing India to now see our ASBO culture, tabloid voyeurism and 'reality TV' obsessions too.

It's a shame we don't view Britain as the Indians do and aspire to those lofty ideals.

The other legacy left by the British was Partition. The reverberations of those traumatic times are most acutely felt in the ongoing dispute over Kashmir, which is largely political and strategic. It is obvious that the root of this enmity was the haphazard manner with which the border was drawn, leaving all too little time for a sensible and ordered transition and for which millions of innocent citizens paid the price.

On my return to my father's ancestral village in Pakistan, I was met with as much warmth and hospitality from the Pakistani Punjabis as I have always been accorded by the Indian Punjabis. The people, it

seems, don't really wish to hate or mistrust each other; it's just that the political culture tells them to.

Travelling around India now as a family man, I realize I've embraced more fully than ever the attributes I've inherited from my family and culture – the joys of the extended family I've created in Britain by incorporating my brothers-in-law and my closest friends into it. I've come to realize that for Indians the relation is the key, and that knows no physical parameters such as distance or time. As a British Indian, I have the best of both worlds, being able to cherry-pick the finest facets of both cultures: the power of individualism and introspection from the West and the virtues of community from the East.

I've also learned more about myself through retracing my parents' odyssey than I ever thought possible, gaining a profound new respect for them and their generation. Every parent should document their life story to be passed on down through the generations; no life is irrelevant. India, by hurling all that life has to offer in your face, all of the time, does make you feel connected in a way that I've never experienced anywhere else. So I guess I now feel a more ardent member of the human race.

The staff at the Virgin check-in desk are helpful and conscientious. In many ways, they strike me as the perfect transition example: Indian faces in the uniform of a successful western company. I settle into my seat in the aircraft and immediately plug in my iPod. *Elvis: The '68 Comeback Special* and, appropriately, 'If I Can Dream'. Perfect. I drift off, allowing the myriad images of my journey to wash over me and merge with the faces of my family, friends and, no doubt, household bills, all waiting for me back in London.

Do you remember the feeling when you see a great magic trick? You're amazed at the skill, the surprise and the execution. Part of the joy is wondering how it's done. Once you know well … it's not magic anymore. India is like a magic trick and perhaps it's best not to know how it's done; maybe we shouldn't try too hard to deconstruct it. Just enjoy the magic.

ACKNOWLEDGEMENTS

An undertaking of this size is the result of a lot of work by a lot of people for a long time – more than five years have passed since we first started dreaming about this project. Thanks to all of you. You know who you are.

I shall spare you a list of people you don't know, but there are a few outstanding individuals that I'd like to thank: Tom Archer at the BBC for seeing the possibilities, and Kate Slattery for making them possible. Also the crews and support staff across Britain, India and Pakistan who made our trip so memorable and kept us out of jail, and the production team who dealt with the endless trail of paperwork generated by our journey.

I would like to thank profoundly all the contributors on this journey for their generosity, wisdom and humour in all their interviews, but particularly 'Papaji' and 'Mama' – the Bhaskar family in Karnal, who revisited a time in their own history that they had tried to protect me from as I was growing up.

After the shooting stops, the cutting begins - and the post-production work of our editors, Stuart Davies, George Farley and the team at Wounded Buffalo, transformed the resulting films from awkward ducklings into beautiful swans. Many thanks.

Infinite respect also goes to DarkHorse FX for producing intricate maps and hypnotic graphics out of thin air; Sunny Sehgal and the boys from Avatar for the sublime soundtrack to the series; and to Sally Potter, Katy Carrington and all at HarperCollins for their infinite patience, good humour and promises of champagne in producing this book, all of which kept me going.

My friend and producer, Deep Sehgal, without whom I could and would not have done this documentary or book, has asked me to thank his family. I want to thank him for being consistently creative and compassionate through every stage of this project.

Finally, I want to thank my parents for allowing me to become a witness to their incredible journey and for being starstruck with me long before anyone else was; my sister and cousin who were my only family in Britain; my friends who continue to define me; and Meera, Milli and Shaan for coping when I was away and coping with me when I was at home, and for making me try to be the best person I possibly can be every day.

Sanjeev Bhaskar
London, 2007

PICTURE CREDITS

4 Corners Images: title page (Massimo Borchi), 16-17 (SIME/Aldo Pavan), 70 (SIME/MassimoRipani), 76-77 (SIME/Riccardo Spila), 151 (SIME/Hans-Peter Huber, 157 (SIME/Hans-Peter Huber), 208-9 (Massimo Borchi), 248 (Massimo Borchi), 283 (SIME/Fridmar Damm); **Alamy**: 131 (Nigel Hicks), 152 (Maciej Wojtkowiak), 168 (Ross McArthur), 264 (David Noble Photography), 275 (Dinodia Images); **Axiom**: 69 (Chris Caldicott), 100 (Chris Caldicott), 128-9 (Francis Bacon), 144 (Jon Spaull), 164 (Chris Caldicott), 177 (Chris Caldicott), 182 (Chris Caldicott), 188 (Chris Caldicott), 202-3 (Dinesh Khanna), 210 (Giles Caldicott), 214 (Giles Caldicott); **Sanjeev Bhaskar**: 9, 15 top, 39 right, 46, 47, 54, 105 right, 116, 167, 172, 173 all, 180, 181, 184, 185, 213; **Corbis**: 20 (Catherine Karnow), 21 (Abraham Nowitz), 30 (Martin Jones), 34-5 (epa), 48-9 (Jagadeesh N.V./REUTERS), 51 left (Manjunath Kiran/epa), 73 (Jeremy Horner), 75 (Barnabas Bosshart), 78 (Jayanta Shaw/REUTERS), 106-7 (Hans Georg Roth), 117 (RicErgenbright), 142-3 (Lindsay Hebberd), 204 (Anthony Cassidy/JAI), 225 (Raminder Pal Singh/epa); **© Dinodia/LinkIndia**: 262 left & right (Anil Dave); **Getty Images**: 13 (Dream Pictures), 14 (Glen Allison), 31 (Sebastian D'Souza/AFP), 50 left (Walter Bibikow), 50 right (Walter Bibikow), 61 (Philip Reeve), 62 (Brooke Slezac), 63 (Neil Emmerson), 66-7(Andrea Booher), 125 (Andrea Pistolesi), 132 (Art Wolfe), 160-1 (Panoramic Images), 166 (Panoramic Images), 250 (Bruno Morandi/Robert Harding); **Robert Harding**: 113 (Sybil Sassoon), 127 (Gavin Hellier), 254 (John Wilson), 266-7 (John Wilson); **Impact Photos**: 120 (Spectrum), 169 (Michael Good), 217 left (Robin Laurence), 217 right (Javed A. Jafferji); **© Link**: 216 left & right (Orde Eliason); **© LinkIndia**:

86 (Dinodia), 99 (Paul Quayle), 103 (Rupert Sagar-Musgrave), 119 (George Torode), 124 (George Torode), 178-9 (Dinodia), 195 (Dinodia), 199 (Dinodia), 218 (Rupert Sagar-Musgrave); **Lonely Planet Images**: 18 (Karen Trist), 148 (Anders Blomqvist), 186 (Greg Elms), 285 (Paul Beinssen); **courtesy of Magarpatta City**: 271 left & right; **On Asia**: 29 (Rajat Ghosh), 51 right (India Today), 80 (Alf Berg), 236 (Siddharth Jain), 260 (Aroon Thaewchatturat), 276 (Agustinus Wibowo), 281 (Sanjit Das); **Deep Sehgal**: 15 bottom, 26, 27, 36, 37, 56, 58, 68, 74, 81 right, 88, 105 left, 112, 114, 135, 137 left & right, 152 right, 153 left & right, 183, 212 all, 221, 232 left, 235, 258, 259; **Reuters Pictures**: 22 (Jayanta Shaw), 25 (Sherwin Crasto), 41 (Prashanth Vishwanathan), 42 (Jagadeesh N.V.), 64-5, 81 (Jayanta Shaw), 82 (Parth Sanyal), 87 (Jayanta Shaw), 89 (Jayanta Shaw), 91 (Jayanta Shaw), 92 (Parth Sanyal), 94-5 (Ajay Verma), 138 (Kamal Kishore), 139 (Raj Patidar), 155 (Fayaz Kabli), 158-9 (B. Mathur), 193 (Ajay Verma), 224 (Kamal Kishore), 268 (Jayanta Shaw); **© 2007 Virgin Comics, LLC. All rights reserved**: 55; **Simon Weller**: 8, 227, 231, 232 left & right, 232 right, 240-241, 242, 246-247 all, 253, 280.

(All pictures are copyright of the photographer unless otherwise indicated.)

pp2–3: Man Mandir Palace and walls, Gwalior Fort, Madhya Pradesh.
pp16–17: Chhatradi temple, Bhuj, Gujerat.
pp76–77: Pushkar city and lake, Rajasthan.
pp142–143: Kaziranga National Park, Assam.
pp208–209: View from the Wind Palace, Jaipur, Rajasthan.